WARRIOR • 163

SPARTAN WARRIOR 735–331 BC

DUNCAN B CAMPBELL

ILLUSTRATED BY STEVE NOON

Series editor Marcus Cowper

First published in Great Britain in 2012 by Osprey Publishing,
PO Box 883, Oxford, OX1 9PL, UK
PO Box 3985, New York, NY 10185-3985, USA
Email: info@ospreypublishing.com

Osprey Publishing is part of the Osprey Group.

Transferred to digital print on demand 2014

First published 2012
2nd impression 2013

Printed and bound by PrintOnDemand-Worldwide.com,
Peterborough, UK

A CIP catalogue record for this book is available from the
British Library

ISBN: 978 1 84908 700 1

Editorial by Ilios Publishing Ltd, Oxford, UK
(www.iliospublishing.com)
Page layout by Mark Holt
Index by Sharon Redmayne
Originated by PDQ Media, Bungay, UK
Typeset in Sabon and Myriad Pro

The Woodland Trust

Osprey Publishing is supporting the Woodland Trust,
the UK's leading woodland conservation charity, by funding
the dedication of trees.

www.ospreypublishing.com

Acknowledgements

It is a pleasure to acknowledge the kindness and generosity of
friends and colleagues, old and new, who sent offprints of
difficult-to-obtain articles or provided illustrations. In particular,
I should like to mention Sandra Petrie Hachey, who facilitated
the reproduction of the fine *calyx-krater* in the collection of the
Davis Museum and Cultural Center; Dr Paraskevi Yiouni, who
sent the image of the splendid Dodona statuette in the
Archaeological Museum of Ioannina; and Stefanos
Skarmintzos, who kindly scoured the museums of Greece for
appropriate photographs.

Dedication

To my friend Dr Peter Wiggins, an expert in most things… except
the Spartans.

A Note on Greek spelling

The transliteration of Greek names and technical terms into
English always presents difficulties. Here, I have attempted to
respect the original language of the Greeks without being
unduly pedantic. I do not like the system of Latin transcription
that converts *perioikoi*, for instance, into *perioeci*. Equally, the
likes of Kleomenes and Archidamos should not, in my opinion,
be renamed Cleomenes and Archidamus. Nevertheless, the
vigilant reader will find that I have applied the rule inconsistently
(e.g. Herodotos, rather than Herodotus, but Aristotle, instead of
Aristoteles). The list of abbreviations and the glossary at the
end of this book should clarify any ambiguities of terminology.

Artist's note

Readers may care to note that the original paintings from which
the colour plates in this book were prepared are available for
private sale. All reproduction copyright whatsoever is retained
by the Publishers. All enquiries should be addressed to:

www.steve-noon.co.uk

The Publishers regret that they can enter into no
correspondence upon this matter.

CONTENTS

SPARTAN WARRIOR 735–331 BC

INTRODUCTION

The largest city-state in ancient Greece was centred, not on a grand metropolis, but on a group of villages along the fertile banks of the river Eurotas. This was Sparta. Her territory, the low-lying 'hollow land' of Lakedaimon, was hedged on either side by mountains, Taygetos to the west and Parnon to the east, but, through conquest, soon stretched from coast to coast across the whole of the southern Peloponnese.

This expansion was achieved, in particular, by the annexation of Messenia, the rich agricultural land that lay across the high Taygetos range. The Messenians, very much second-class citizens in their own land, never

View of the modern town of Sparti and the Taygetos Mountains from the east. In the foreground lie the ruins of the later Roman theatre. Little survives of Classical Sparta. (Wikimedia Commons/ Ulrich Still)

forgot their stolen freedom and are often represented as Sparta's enemy within. It is entirely fitting that the poetry of the famous bard Tyrtaios, which represents almost the sum total of Spartan literature, was inspired by a Messenian War.

The 'town' of Sparta consisted, not of a gradually built-up city, but of a collection of villages (more correctly known by the Spartan term *obai*, or 'obes'): Pitana, home of the Agiad kings; Limnai, home of the Eurypontid kings; Mesoa and Kynosoura; and nearby Amyklai. Outlying communities were inhabited by so-called *perioikoi* (literally 'those who live round about', memorably named the 'circum-residents' by the great 19th-century historian George Grote). All of these owed allegiance to Sparta and could be called up for military service in support of her citizen hoplites.

Far more numerous were the helots, rent-paying country folk forced to labour in the fields so that the landowners, the pure-bred men of Sparta (the so-called Spartiates), could concentrate on their military lifestyle. Spartan relations with this rural population remain enigmatic, but have often been seen as troubled. The Oxford historian G. B. Grundy memorably conjured an image of the Spartans 'holding, as it were, a wolf by the throat'. But the helots were little different from the servile rural populations of other city-states who employed similar unfree labour.

Map of the Peloponnese, showing the sites of major battles mentioned in the text. (Author's collection)

Lykourgos the law-giver

At some point in the 8th century, traditionally 776 BC, a lawgiver named Lykourgos laid down the constitution, the so-called Great Rhetra, obtained from the Delphic oracle of Apollo, by which the Spartans would live. Or so the story goes. Herodotos certainly believed that 'Lykourgos established Sparta's military institutions: the *enomotiai* and the *triekades* and the *syssitia*; and, in addition to these, the ephors and *gerontes*' (Hdt. 1.65.5). (All technical terms are explained in the Glossary.)

Later writers and thinkers (such as Polybius, Plutarch and Pausanias, all writing during the Roman period) believed that the god-given customs of the Spartan people had remained unchanged since that time. The Spartans, in Cicero's words, were 'the only men in the whole world who have lived now for more than 700 years with one and the same set of customs and unchanging laws' (Cic., *Flacc.* 63).

We now know that Cicero was mistaken. The 3rd-century reforming kings, Agis IV and Kleomenes III, instituted changes to Spartan society, but opinion is divided about their precise nature. Nevertheless, most are agreed that further change came after the Roman conquest of Greece in 146 BC. For this reason, we should use the testimony of later writers sparingly, since it is arguable that they were describing a post-reformation Sparta, a Sparta that had reinvented itself to please Roman tourists.

On the other hand, the views of Herodotos, Thukydides, Plato, Xenophon and Aristotle should be privileged, because they wrote their respective works before any major change occurred, and Plutarch may be used with care, because he seems to have conducted personal research 'in the Lakedaimonian public records' (Plut., *Ages.* 19.6).

Spartan government

Sparta was ruled by the curious phenomenon of a dyarchy, whereby two royal houses – the Agiad and the Eurypontid, both descended from Zeus via Herakles – each supplied a king. Xenophon explains that Lykourgos ordained that the kings, 'being of divine descent, should perform all public sacrifices on behalf of the city-state, and should lead the army wherever the city-state sends it' (Xen., *Lak. pol.* 15.2). However, their powers were circumscribed by the 28 *gerontes* ('elders') who sat alongside them in the *gerousia* to make the decisions of state, while Spartiates over the age of 30 had the right of regular assembly in the *ekklesia*.

As a counterbalance to the *gerousia*, a committee of five ephors was elected annually from the *ekklesia* using an oral voting system which Aristotle found 'childish' (Arist., *Pol.* 2.9 = 1270ʙ). Any Spartan warrior who had not already served as ephor might find himself co-opted for a year, so it was important that his education had prepared him for the various domestic, foreign, and judicial responsibilities of the post, which included mustering the army.

Spartan society

Plutarch claims that there were originally 9,000 *kleroi*, the allotments of land parcelled out, one per Spartiate, to support each man's household. However, no Spartiate required his own allotment until he joined one of the mess-groups known as *syssitia* at the age of 20, and perhaps not even then, if the mess contributions were waived for those under the age of 30.

The precise nature of these *kleroi* has proved an intractable problem for generations of scholars. Plutarch implies that all Spartan land was equally divided into allotments which, once assigned to their owners, could not be divided, disposed of, or added to. This is almost certainly wrong, for it seems that 'their lawgiver (Lykourgos) quite rightly made it dishonourable to buy and sell land in someone's possession, but allowed anyone to transfer it to others by gift or bequest' (Arist., *Pol.* 2.9 = 1270A). This system naturally produced great inequality amongst the so-called *homoioi* ('equals'). Aristotle observed that, 'if many are born and the land is divided accordingly, many must inevitably become poor' (Arist., *Pol.* 2.9 = 1270B); in other words, if a man had several heirs, his *kleros* would need to be broken up, giving each son a smaller allotment.

This was a particular problem in a society where the begetting of sons was positively encouraged, for the father of three sons was apparently excused military service and the father of four sons paid no taxes. Daughters' dowries could redress the situation somewhat, as each bride appears likely to have inherited part of her father's *kleros*, which was thus transferred to her new husband. But many men might find that their *kleros* was a fraction of the size of their father's. As we shall see, this could pose a problem for the Spartan warrior.

Marble bust of the Athenian writer Xenophon, who knew King Agesilaos personally. On his exile from Athens (*c.*394 BC), he settled in the Peloponnese and sent his two sons to be educated at Sparta. (Now in the Bibliotheca Alexandrina Antiquities Museum, Egypt. Photo © Daniel P. Diffendale)

The Spartan population

Despite the Lykourgan encouragement to procreate, it is generally agreed that the number of Spartiates gradually declined, from the 6th-century heyday, when they numbered almost 10,000, to the *oliganthropia* ('shortage of men') which Aristotle observed as the cause of Sparta's catastrophic decline in the 4th century BC. Unfortunately, demographic studies of ancient Sparta are hampered, not only by the scarcity of evidence, but also by the inveterate Spartan tendency towards secrecy. Even its kings were not above manipulating the truth; on one occasion, Agesilaos reported a Spartan defeat to his men as a victory, on the grounds that 'there was no need to share bad tidings with them' (Xen., *Hell.* 4.3.13). Both Thukydides and Pausanias ran into trouble trying to estimate battle casualties, the latter noting that 'the Spartans were always inclined to conceal their mishaps' (Paus. 9.13.11; cf. Plut., *Ap. Bas.*, *Epam.* 12 = *Mor.* 193B, on Leuktra; cf. Thuk. 5.68.2, on Mantineia).

At Plataia in 479 BC, 5,000 Spartiates took the field, accompanied by an equal number of *perioikoi*, and an astonishing 35,000 helots. The historian G. B. Grundy assumed that these 5,000 Spartiates represented the total able-bodied male population aged between 20 and 50, but Herodotos indicates that the 5,000 were *neotes* ('young men'), a term that seems inappropriate for men as old as 50.

In any case, he also claimed that 'Sparta is a town of around 8,000 men' (Hdt. 7.234.2).

This total was naturally eroded by constant warfare and the Spartan tradition of demoting any citizen who had shown cowardice in the face of danger, or whose landholdings were insufficient to support him in the lifestyle of a full-time hoplite warrior. The great earthquake of 464 BC also took its toll. Plutarch records that 'the land of Lakedaimon was ripped into many chasms by quite the greatest earthquake in living memory and many of Taygetos' peaks were shaken down, so that the very town was obliterated except for five houses, as the earthquake demolished all the others' (Plut., *Kim*. 16.4).

The fate of any land left ownerless by the disaster is unknown, but the shadowy section of the Spartan population known as the *neodamodeis* ('new men of the people') was perhaps created at this time to take over any vacant *kleroi*. These are thought to have been freed helots, because the historian Myron of Priene records that 'the Spartans often freed their slaves' and, after listing the various names for them, claims that 'others are called *neodamodeis*, being different from helots' (Athen., *Deipn*. 6.102 = 271F). These pseudo-*perioikoi* were, like them, liable for military service, although the first recorded instance of this is not until 421 BC.

By then, matters must have become very serious, for Thukydides suggests that there were only about 2,800 Spartiates at Mantineia in 418 BC, a surprisingly small total given that a full mobilization had been ordered. Two generations later, there were only 700 Spartiates available for service at Leuktra and only 300 of them survived the battle (Xen., *Hell*. 6.4.15). By then, the heyday of the Spartan warrior had passed.

CHRONOLOGY

The reigns of Spartan kings are indicated in italics; *(A)* indicates an Agiad king; *(E)* indicates a Eurypontid king

776 BC	Lykourgos lays down Spartan law
c.760 BC	*Reign of Archelaos (A) and Charillos (E)*
735–715 BC	First Messenian War
c.720 BC	*Reign of Polydoros (A) and Theopompos (E)*
706 BC	Foundation of Spartan colony at Taras (Tarentum)
669 BC	Battle of Hysiai, Sparta defeated by Argos
650–630 BC	Second Messenian War
c.640 BC	Tyrtaios writes his poetry
c.575 BC	*Reign of Leon (A) and Agasikles (E)*
c.545 BC	'Battle of the Champions' (Sparta defeats Argos at Thyrea)

*c.*530 BC	*Reign of Anaxandridas II (A) and Ariston (E)*
525 BC	Spartan siege of Samos fails
*c.*510 BC	*Reign of Kleomenes I (A) and Demaratos (E)*
506 BC	Spartan invasion of Attica
494 BC	Battle of Sepeia, Sparta defeats Argos
491–469 BC	*Reign of Leotychidas II (E)*
490–480 BC	*Reign of Leonidas I (A)*
490 BC	Third Messenian War (disputed by some scholars) Sparta misses battle of Marathon
480 BC	Battle of Thermopylai (Spartan defeat delays Persian invasion)
480–458 BC	*Reign of Pleistarchos (A)*
480–469 BC	*Regency of Pausanias (A)*
479 BC	Battle of Plataia (Spartan-led confederation defeats Persian army)
469–427 BC	*Reign of Archidamos II (E)*
*c.*469 BC	Battle of Tegea (Spartans defeat Tegeans and Argives)
465 BC	Great earthquake at Sparta
*c.*464 BC	Fourth (or Third) Messenian War Battle of Stenykleros (Spartans defeated by Messenians)
*c.*464 BC	Battle of Dipaia (Spartans defeat Arkadians)
458–408 BC	*Reign of Pleistoanax (A) (in exile, 446/5–427/6)*
457 BC	Battle of Tanagra (Spartan army narrowly defeats the Athenians)
445 BC	Thirty Years Peace with Athens
431–421 BC	Archidamian War (first stage of Peloponnesian War with Athens), Sparta invades Attika in 431, 430, 428, 427 and 425
429–427 BC	Siege of Plataia (Spartans capture town)
427–400 BC	*Reign of Agis II (E)*
425 BC	Incident on Sphakteria (Spartan force surrenders to Athenians)
422 BC	Battle of Amphipolis (Spartans defeat Athenians)

418 BC	Battle of Mantineia (Spartans defeat Athenian-led coalition)
413 BC	Spartans occupy Dekeleia in Attika
412 BC	Spartan alliance with Persia
408–395 BC	*Reign of Pausanias (A)*
405 BC	Battle of Aigospotamoi (Spartan fleet defeats Athenians)
404 BC	Fall of Athens signals end of Peloponnesian War
401 BC	Xenophon leads the 'Ten Thousand' mercenaries from Persia to the Black Sea
400–360 BC	*Reign of Agesilaos II (E)*
395–380 BC	*Reign of Agesipolis I (A)*
395 BC	Corinthian War (conflict between Sparta and a Corinthian-led coalition)
395 BC	Battle of Haliartos (Spartans defeated by Theban-led coalition)
394 BC	Battle of Nemea (Spartans defeat Corinthian-led coalition) Battle of Koroneia (Spartans defeat Theban-led coalition) Battle of Knidos (Spartan fleet defeated by Athenian–Persian coalition)
392 BC	Battle of the Long Walls of Corinth (Spartans defeat Corinthian and Theban forces)
390 BC	Battle of Lechaion (Spartans defeated by Athenians)
386 BC	The King's Peace ends the Corinthian War
385 BC	Siege and capture of Mantineia by the Spartans
380–371 BC	*Reign of Kleombrotos I (A)*
375 BC	Battle of Tegyra (Sparta defeated by Thebes)
371–370 BC	*Reign of Agesipolis II (A)*
371 BC	Battle of Leuktra (Sparta defeated by Thebes)
370 BC	Liberation of Messenia from Sparta
370–309 BC	*Reign of Kleomenes (A)*
368 BC	Tearless Battle (Spartans defeat Arkadian-led coalition)

364 BC	Battle of Kromnos (Spartans defeated by Arkadian-led coalition)
362 BC	Agesilaos successfully defends Sparta against Theban invasion Second battle of Mantineia (Athenian–Spartan coalition defeated by Thebans)
360–338 BC	*Reign of Archidamos III (E)*
355–346 BC	Third Sacred War
338–331 BC	*Reign of Agis III (E)*
331 BC	Battle of Megalopolis (Sparta defeated by Macedon)

TRAINING AND EDUCATION

Sparta differed from other Greek city-states in many ways, the most radical of which was the institution of the unique education system known as the *agoge*. By taking over all Spartan boys' lives for 23 years, it 'prepared them to follow commands willingly, to persevere with toil, and to conquer in battle' (Plut., *Lyk.* 16.6). Above all, it instilled conformity in every Spartiate, and taught (in the words of King Agesilaos) 'the finest lesson, which is to rule and to be ruled' (Plut., *Ap. Lak.*, *Ages.* 50–51 = *Mor.* 212B–C; *Ages.* 20.2). Only in this way were the Spartiates truly *homoioi* ('equals'), having endured the same initiation course.

Marble bust of the philosopher Aristotle, pupil of Plato and tutor of Alexander the Great. His vast and eclectic writings included works on political theory, including a lost work on *The Spartan Constitution*. (Now in the Museo Nazionale Romano, Rome. Wikimedia Commons/Marie-Lan Nguyen)

The importance of the *agoge* was paramount. In 331 BC, after the Spartan defeat at Megalopolis, the ephor Eteokles refused to comply with the Macedonian demand for 50 children as hostages, 'in case the boys turned out to be uneducated through missing the traditional *agoge*' (Plut., *Ap. Lak.*, *Anon.* 54 = *Mor.* 235B).

The training of boys

Xenophon drew a distinction between Sparta and the rest of Greece on three counts: first, Greek children were normally handed into the care of an educated slave as their tutor (*paidagogos*); second, Greek children were normally provided with sandals and changes of clothing; and third, Greek children were normally given a sufficiency of food. The Spartans did none of these things.

Between the ages of seven and (probably) 12, Spartan boys ('*paides*') underwent a specific training regime, under the overall supervision of a warden called the *paidonomos* (literally 'herder of boys'). This was a highly respected Spartan, drawn from the highest social class, in stark contrast to the employment of servile *paidagogoi* in other city-states. His authority allowed him to

Marble life-size statue of a warrior excavated at Sparta in 1925. Although the arms are missing, archaeologists found the right foot and the left leg (not illustrated), which wears a decorated greave. From its estimated date of 470 BC, it has been suggested that the statue posthumously portrayed King Leonidas. (Now in Sparta Museum. Photo © Stefanos Skarmintzos)

punish any who misbehaved, and to this end he was accompanied by a whip-wielding squad of youths to mete out his punishments. The net result, according to Xenophon, was that 'great respect and great obedience are found' (Xen., *Lak. pol.* 2.2) at Sparta.

As befits a system that was ultimately designed to produce effective warriors, great emphasis was placed on a rough-and-tumble lifestyle. The boys were divided into bands (*agelai*, literally 'herds') and they chose as their leader the boy who was 'the most resolute at fighting' (Plut., *Lyk.* 16.5). All the time, in addition to the *paidonomos*, the older Spartan men kept an eye on their antics, punishing disobedience and encouraging competition.

Boys were not permitted to wear shoes. The reasoning behind this, as Xenophon explains, was that 'leaping, jumping and running were accomplished more swiftly barefoot, if a boy trained his feet that way, than wearing shoes' (Xen., *Lak. pol.* 2.3). Not only was the Spartan warrior guaranteed to be sure-footed, but his feet were hardened from an early age. Likewise, the boys were permitted only one cloak throughout the year, rather than switching between summer and winter garments, so that they would grow accustomed to heat and cold, and would be used to making do.

Food was rationed for two reasons. Lykourgos apparently thought that 'a diet that produces slim bodies would do more to increase height than one that fattened them with food' (Xen., *Lak. pol.* 2.5). However, more importantly, a restricted diet enhanced certain key skills: the ability to perform effectively on an empty stomach, for example, or simply to subsist on rations for longer. Plutarch develops the point of the starvation diet in his *Customs of the Spartans*: 'for they thought that they would be more useful in war', he writes, 'if they were able to persevere without food' (Plut., *Inst. Lac.* 13 = *Mor.* 237F). Equally, being inured to a plain diet meant that the Spartan could subsist on anything that came to hand.

The rationing of food was accompanied by the condoning of theft, provided the object was to gather foodstuffs. Again, there was good military logic behind the practice, for 'it is clear that anyone wishing to steal must stay awake at night, and must be wily and remain on the lookout during the day, and anyone wishing to seize anything must post lookouts' – all sound military principles (Xen., *Lak. pol.* 2.7). A fragment of Aristotle's lost *Spartan Constitution* explains that the goal was to produce warriors who were 'better able to endure fatigue and lack of sleep in the face of the enemy' (Frg. 611). Moreover, by stealing foodstuffs, the boys were honing the foraging skills of the warrior on campaign. And there were other lessons to be learned from stealing:

> When the time came for the boys to steal whatever they could, and it was shameful to be found out, some boys stole a young fox alive and gave it to a particular boy to keep. When those who had lost the fox came along in search of it, it so happened that, as the boy had slipped it under his cloak, the beast was enraged and savaged his side through to the vital organs, but the boy remained motionless, so as not to be found out. Later, when they had gone away, the boys saw what had happened and scolded him, saying that it would have been better to reveal the fox than to hide it with fatal results; but the boy said, 'Not at all: better to die without giving in to the pain than to preserve your life dishonourably, having been detected through weakness'. (Plut., *Ap. Lak., Anon.* 35 = *Mor.* 234A–B)

Stealing was character-forming. Clearly, it was shameful to be caught in the act, because that implied a lack of skill. Xenophon explains that, 'when people are teaching, they punish those who do not follow instruction properly; so the Spartans punish those who are caught on account of being inept at stealing' (Xen., *Lak. pol.* 2.8). The penalty, according to Plutarch, was a beating.

Of course, the basics of education were not neglected. Plutarch writes that, 'by placing them under the same discipline and mealtimes, Lykourgos accustomed them to play together and study together' (Plut., *Lyk.* 16.4). To be sure, he explains elsewhere that 'education trained them in happily following commands, patiently enduring toil, and either prevailing in battle or dying' (Plut., *Inst. Lac.* 4 = *Mor.* 237A). But they also learned to read and write, and, although Plutarch claims that this was purely utilitarian, the Spartans were known for their love of music, poetry and dance. Indeed, later writers believed that the war dance known as the *pyrrhiche*, which 'includes the motions executed to avoid blows and shots of all kinds' (Pl., *Leg.* 815A), had been invented at Sparta.

The training of older boys

Spartan boys were divided according to year groups, and Plutarch emphasizes the age of 12 as a watershed in every Spartan's education. Each band of *paidiskoi* (or 'little boys', surely an ironic title) now lived and trained together under the supervision of a selected *eiren* ('prefect') drawn from the ranks of the youths. Xenophon says that responsibility for each band (he calls them *ilai*, literally 'crowds') was given to the smartest of the *eirenes*, but Plutarch claims that it was 'the most cunning and battle-ready *eiren*' (Plut., *Lyk.* 17.2; cf. Xen., *Lak. pol.* 2.11). The boys were obliged to give him their blind obedience, respect his decisions, and endure his punishments.

Moreover, they had to act as his servants at mealtimes, collecting firewood and fetching vegetables using their thieving skills. After dinner, the boys were expected to entertain him, but everything had a didactic purpose, as Plutarch explains:

Scene from a red-figure *kylix* (wine cup), depicting *ephebes* (the equivalent of the Spartan *hebontes*) equipping themselves for war. The bearded youth in the centre carries a folded fabric corslet. (From E. Gerhard, *Auserlesene griechische Vasenbilder*, Vol. 4, Berlin, 1858, Tafel 29)

As he reclined after dinner, the *eiren* would order one of the boys to sing, while to another he posed a question requiring a considered answer; for instance, 'Who is the best amongst the men?' or 'What do you think about this man's success?' In this way, they were accustomed to judging excellence and appraising the other citizens right from the start; for, when asked which citizen was good, or which one was dishonourable, any who had no answer were considered slothful, and their soul showed no ambition for excellence. (Plut., *Lyk.* 18.2)

Clearly, the training of the *paidiskoi* became full-time, as Xenophon reckoned that the laws of Lykourgos 'imposed the maximum labours and contrived the longest tasks' for these boys (Xen., *Lak. pol.* 3.2). They learned to conduct themselves with modesty, and to speak only when spoken to.

Whether or not the younger *paides* returned to their homes at night, the *paidiskoi* certainly did not, for they began sleeping in barracks on makeshift mattresses (*stibades*) that they manufactured from reeds and straw. It was probably for cutting and gathering this bedding material that the boys carried a small sickle called a *xyele*. Whatever the reason for this tradition, its military application is obvious. Less obvious is the reasoning behind their nudity, for Plutarch records that, not only did they exercise naked, but 'from the age of 12 they never wore a tunic and were given only one cloak a year' (Plut., *Lyk.* 16.6), further emphasizing that all were *homoioi* ('equals').

Also at the age of 12, the *paidiskos* was taken under the wing of an *erastes* ('admirer') as his *eromenos* ('beloved'), to receive a form of mentoring. In other Greek city-states, it was quite normal for an older man to take a youngster as his companion, but the relationship was normally a sexual one. Not so in Sparta. Desire for the *eromenos*' body rather than concern for his 'soul', or moral upbringing, was thought to be shameful.

Once he reached the age of 18 or 19, when other Greek boys left their education behind, the Spartan *paidiskos* progressed to the next landmark in the *agoge*, becoming a *melleiren*, a title which means 'nearly an *eiren*'. He was now on the threshold of youth.

The training of youths

A Spartan reached his youth (*hebe*) at the age of 20, when he became liable for military service. However, as a *hebon*, he was not yet a full citizen; in many Greek city-states, 30 was the age of full responsibility, and it seems to have been no different in Sparta, for the *hebontes* were still answerable to the *paidonomos*, whose supervision ceased only on the *hebon*'s 30th birthday.

Xenophon explains that, in general, the Lykourgan system was designed to make the *hebontes* 'achieve manly virtue' (Xen., *Lak. pol.* 4.2). Nevertheless, as *neoi* ('youths') who were not yet adults, they were also obliged to submit to periodic inspections; the writer Agatharchides records that 'every ten days the youths had to stand naked before the ephors' (Athen., *Deipn.* 12.550c) as a check on obesity, because the *hebontes* were responsible for their own exercising. The ephors also inspected their clothing and bedding every day in their barracks. Furthermore, it was the right of any Spartan citizen to challenge any *hebon*'s movements 'and to strike any who did not answer or who contrived an excuse' (Plut., *Inst. Lak.* 8 = *Mor.* 237c).

One duty specifically laid upon the new *hebontes* was the provision of *eirenes* ('prefects') to look after the *agelai* of boys, but this seems to have lasted for only one year; otherwise, the constant supervision of boys would have prevented the youths from spending any time at all with the adult Spartans. Naturally, the *eiren* was, himself, under scrutiny, in particular for the appropriateness of his punishments, perfectly illustrating King Agesilaos' aphorism that the first lesson is to rule and be ruled. Other *hebontes* were required as the *paidonomos*' assistants.

Another duty fulfilled by some *hebontes* was service in the royal bodyguard, known as the *hippeis*. Every year, the ephors named three adult Spartiates as *hippagretai* ('*hippeis* choosers'), each of whom judged the *hebontes* publicly before making his selection of 100 individuals. The 300 thus chosen served for a year. Each *hebon* had only ten opportunities to be chosen, once per year, so competition for enrolment was fierce and it often came to blows between those who were picked and those who were not.

Scene from a black-figure *kylix* by the so-called 'Hunt Painter' (*c.*550–530 BC), depicting Spartans hunting a boar. (Now in the Louvre, Paris. Wikimedia Commons/Marie-Lan Nguyen)

As far as the duties of the *hippeis* were concerned, one of the privileges enjoyed by the Spartan kings was that '100 picked men guard them on campaign' (Hdt. 6.56). Two kings would thus monopolize 200 *hippeis*; the remainder were perhaps deployed for internal security at Sparta.

It seems that, by and large, *hebontes* were too young to take a wife, for Lykourgos insisted that Spartans should marry 'in the prime of manhood' (Xen., *Lak. pol.* 1.6), a phrase which implies 30 or so years of age. This, of course, tallies with our general impression of the treatment of *hebontes* as not quite adult. It also accounts for the rule, that 'the youths under 30 never went to the marketplace, but procured their household necessities through their kinsfolk or *erastai*' (Plut., *Lyk.* 25.1), because otherwise their wives could have fulfilled this function.

Nevertheless, there are few aspects of the Spartan lifestyle which allow certainty, and many would argue that Spartans could, indeed, marry before the age of 30, albeit furtively. Plutarch paints a picture of the new husband, 'spending the day with his peers and sleeping with them', while slipping stealthily into his bride's bed between times (Plut., *Lyk.* 15.4; cf. *Ap. Lak.*, *Lyk.* 17 = *Mor.* 228A); this is clearly the lifestyle of the *hebon*, though perhaps one of the older ones.

It is also worth noting from Plutarch's marketplace comment, that the *hebon* must have continued to maintain the special relationship with the 'admirer' whom he met as a *paidiskos*. Kleonymos, the *eromenos* of the future king Archidamos, was probably a *hebon* of around 22 years of age when 'at Leuktra, fighting in front of the King alongside Deinon the *polemarchos*, he thrice fell' (Xen., *Hell.* 5.4.33), and yet his noble death still brought honour upon his one-time *erastes*.

Xenophon occasionally uses the expression 'the ten from youth' (Xen., *Hell.* 2.4.32; 3.4.23; 4.5.14; 5.4.40; *Ages.* 1.31) to indicate a proportion of the Spartan army. Some have suggested that this cryptic phrase refers to the number of years that have elapsed since the men reached youth (*hebe*);

A Hellenic re-enactor recreates the Spartiate immortalized in the famous 'Draped Warrior' figurine, now in the Wadsworth Atheneum (USA). The significance of the transverse crest is not known, but it perhaps indicates high status. (Photo © Stefanos Skarmintzos. Courtesy of the Hellenic living history club 'Koryvantes': www.koryvantes.org)

by this logic, it would indicate 'men who are 30 years old'. However, it seems more likely that the phrase is simply a circumlocution for *hebontes*, and means 'the ten (year groups) from youth', namely those aged 20 to 29, comprising the younger men whose time in military service was ten years or less.

The Spartan warrior

Once a Spartan had completed the *agoge* and passed from the supervision of the *paidonomos*, he was a fully-fledged Spartiate, as long as he could maintain a place in a *syssition*, or 'mess-group' (see below, p. 38). His role as a Spartan warrior was expected to continue until he became a *geron* at the age of 60 (though some have suggested that he continued to be liable for a further five years' military service)

No ancient writer mentions any specific training regime followed by adult Spartiates. However, the fact that 'it is required by law for all Lakedaimonians to practise gymnastic exercises, even while on campaign' (Xen., *Lak. pol.* 12.5), suggests that the adults trained at other times, as well. The younger adults, at least, were expected to maintain a certain level of fitness, judging from the occasions on which the 30–34-year-olds were ordered into action alongside the *hebontes* as 'the 15 from youth' (Xen., *Hell.* 4.5.16, 6.10).

Moreover, the Spartans' enthusiasm for hunting, to the extent that any Spartiate who lacked his own hunting dogs could expect to borrow those of a neighbour (Xen., *Lak. pol.* 6.2), is not entirely irrelevant to maintaining a high level of military capability. Xenophon claims that Lykourgos encouraged hunting 'so that the men might be able to stand the toil of soldiering as well as the *hebontes* do' (Xen., *Lak. pol.* 4.7).

DRESS AND APPEARANCE

Spartan hair

The iconic image of the Spartan warrior is of a long-haired, bearded individual. These are precisely the aspects emphasized by Plutarch, in his description of a statue of the Spartan Lysander (Plut., *Lys.* 1.1: 'long-haired in the ancient manner and sporting an excellent beard'); and when Alkibiades adopted a Spartan lifestyle, he is described as 'needing a haircut' (Plut., *Alk.* 23.3).

SPARTAN WARRIOR, c.546 BC

This Spartan warrior from the time of the 'Battle of the Champions' is shown wearing the equipment depicted on an archaic Lakonian figurine from Kosmas, in the vicinity of Thyrea (now in the National Archaeological Museum, Athens). Similar archaic figurines, along with the evidence of several vase paintings, confirm that warriors went into battle naked, except for the helmet, 'bell' cuirass (**1**) and greaves (**2**). They are often depicted with high crests on their helmets.

The two styles of helmet shown here are the open-faced 'Illyrian' (**3**) and an early variety of 'Corinthian' (**4**), which introduced the nose guard and covered more of the wearer's face. Both styles could be fitted with crests, either made from horsehair (**5**) or fashioned from bronze (**6**).

The Spartan warrior was a spearman, first and foremost, and is shown with the large hoplite shield (*aspis*) and spear (*dory*). The spearheads and butt-spikes are based on examples in the National Archaeological Museum, Athens. The shield emblem is the Gorgoneion (or Medusa mask) (**7**), a motif that was popular at Sparta, where it recurs on bronzework and on bone and ivory carvings.

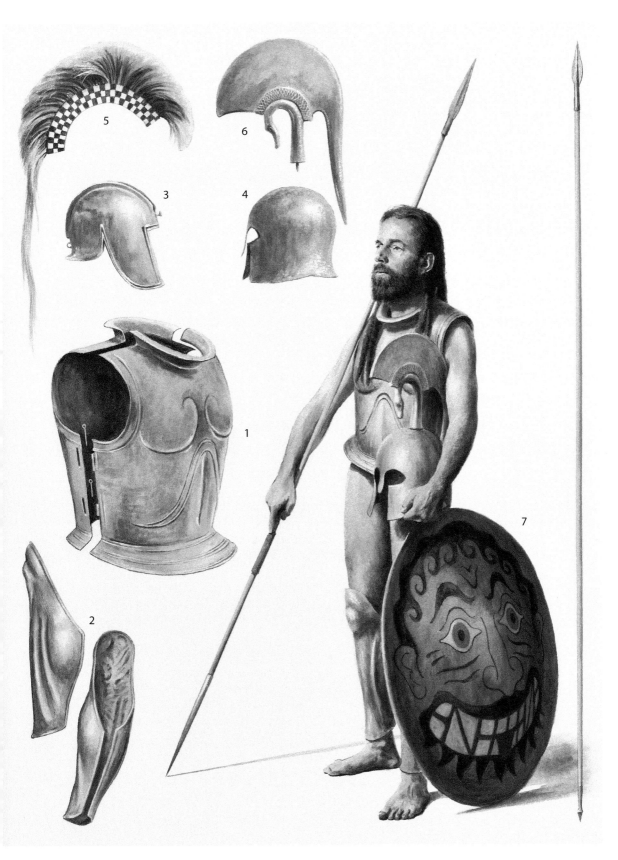

5

6

3

4

1

2

7

However, under the regulations of the *agoge*, Spartan boys wore their hair short. It was only when they reached adulthood and were 'beyond the age of youth' (Xen., *Lak. pol.* 11.3) that they might allow their hair to grow. Plutarch took this to mean that a *hebon* aged 20 could wear his hair long; he specifically wrote that the Spartans were 'long-haired since the age of *ephebeia*' (Plut., *Lyk.* 22.1), the '*ephebes*' of other city-states being broadly equivalent to the 18- or 19-year-old Spartan *melleirenes*. However, Xenophon probably means that a Spartan had to wait until he had progressed 'beyond the age of being a *hebon*'; in other words, the age of 30, as Spartans aged 20–29 were still considered youths.

Long hair was deemed to be both noble and fearsome. But, as with many Spartan traditions, the roots of this one were lost in obscurity. Herodotos dates the custom only as far back as the 'Battle of the Champions' at Thyrea, but Plutarch thought that it was an ancestral tradition. 'The Spartiates took care of their hair because they bore in mind one of Lykourgos' sayings about it', he wrote, 'namely, that it renders handsome men better looking, and ugly ones more frightening' (Plut., *Ap. Lak.*, *Lyk.* 29 = *Mor.* 228F).

The adult Spartan hairstyle sent other subliminal messages. Firstly, frugality; when one of the early Spartan kings, Kharillos, was asked why he wore long hair, he is said to have replied, 'because, out of all the decorations, this one is natural and costs nothing' (Plut., *Ap. Lak.*, *Khar.* 6 = *Mor.* 232D). The second message was freedom from drudgery: Aristotle wrote that 'wearing long hair is honourable in Lakedaimon, for it is the mark of freedom, because it is difficult to do menial labour with long hair' (Arist., *Rhet.* 8.26-27 = 1367A).

RIGHT
Bronze Spartan warrior figurine from the ancient shrine at Dodona. Besides the characteristic long, braided hair, he sports a full moustache and beard. (Now in the Archaeological Museum of Ioannina. Photo © Archaeological Museum of Ioannina, Ministry of Culture and Tourism – TAP)

FAR RIGHT
Bronze figurine of a Spartan warrior. Although bearded, the man does not appear to have a moustache, in compliance with the ephors' annual instruction to 'cut off the *mustax*'. (Now in Olympia Museum. Photo © Daniel P. Diffendale)

It is often imagined that Spartans wore facial hair in a distinctive manner that combined a beard (*geneias*) with a shaven upper lip. Certainly, Plutarch records that 'the ephors, immediately on entering office, as Aristotle says, order the citizens to cut off their *mustax* (moustache) and to obey the laws, so that these may not be harsh' (Plut., *Kleom.* 9.2, with a similar version at *Mor.* 550B). Since no other author refers to this custom, it is difficult to be sure, but it seems that, at least in Aristotle's day, the moustache-shaving was an annual ritual, symbolizing obedience to the laws.

A statue discovered at Sparta in 1925 appears to have a short beard and shaven upper lip (see illustration on page 12), though it has been suggested that, since statuary was invariably painted, the artist had perhaps added a moustache at that stage. Certainly, other evidence suggests that, by and large, the Spartans were proud to wear moustaches. For example, one well-known bronze figurine of a Spartan from the shrine at Dodona sports a full moustache and beard, and the Spartan depicted on the Davis Museum *krater* (illustrated on p. 20) is similarly endowed.

In his comedies, the Athenian writer Aristophanes characterizes Spartans by their *hypene*, a word which modern translators often render as 'beard' (in order to conform to the stereotype of the bearded Spartan), but Aristotle clearly uses *hypene* as a synonym for *mustax*, indicating the moustache (as a counterbalance to the *geneias*, or beard). Furthermore, the playwright Antiphanes, quoted by the Roman writer Athenaeus, sums up the customs of the Spartans (albeit satirically) like this: 'go to the *syssition* for your dinner; enjoy their broth; wear a moustache (*mustax*); do not despise nor wish for other refinements in their customs, but be old-fashioned' (Athen., *Deipn.* 4.21 = 143A).

In fact, the peculiar punishment reserved for those who had shown cowardice in the face of danger included the obligation to 'shave part of their moustache (*hypene*) and allow part of it to grow' (Plut., *Ages.* 30.3). Clearly, a man must already have a moustache in order to shave part of it off; in fact, if the Spartans ritually shaved their moustache once every year to symbolize obedience to the law, it is perhaps fitting that anyone who failed to obey the law (in this case, the prohibition against cowardice) should draw attention to himself by shaving only partially.

Spartan dress

As we have seen, the ban on *paides* wearing shoes was in order to toughen the Spartan warriors' feet, so it is likely that they rarely wore sandals or boots. The Spartan depicted on the Davis Museum *krater*, for example, is barefoot. The Athenian orator Demosthenes scorned his countrymen who 'played the Spartan' by feigning a sullen mood and wearing the *tribon*, a distinctively

Ivory combs from the Sanctuary of Artemis Orthia at Sparta. The Gorgoneion (or mask of Medusa) was a popular motif at Sparta. Now in the National Archaeological Museum, Athens. (Photo © Stefanos Skarmintzos)

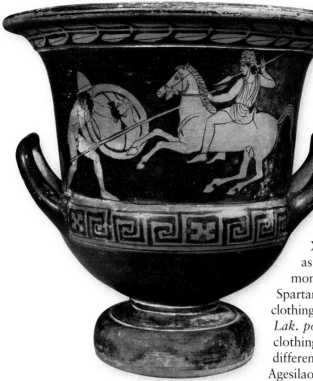

Greek red-figure *krater*, *c.*440–420 BC, depicting the combat between a Spartan hoplite and a cavalryman. The Spartans trapped on Sphakteria in 425 BC were armed in this lightweight fashion. (Now in Davis Museum and Cultural Center, USA. Photo © Davis Museum and Cultural Center, Wellesley College, Wellesley, MA)

Spartan cloak. When the Spartan Gylippos arrived in Syracuse in 414 BC to organize the city's defence, the Athenian attackers characterized him as 'a *tribon* carrying a staff', and completed the stereotype by claiming to have dealt with Spartans 'far sturdier than Gylippos and longer-haired' (Plut., *Nik.* 19.3).

The Spartans had a reputation for dressing simply. Aristotle wrote that 'the rich wear clothes which any poor man would be able to procure' (Arist., *Pol.* 4.9 = 1294B), as proof of their egalitarian society of *homoioi* ('equals'). For Xenophon, it wasn't so much about the equality, as about Spartan pride: 'There is no need to make money for spending on fine cloaks, because Spartans are admired not for the extravagance of their clothing, but for the healthy state of their bodies' (Xen., *Lak. pol.* 7.3). The net result was the same: Spartan clothing created a unifying bond that cut across any differences in wealth or status. In 360 BC, when King Agesilaos, by then in his eighties, arrived in Egypt with 30 Spartiates to support the Pharaoh against Persia, the Egyptians were surprised to see 'an old man, his body small and lean, wrapped in a coarse, shabby cloak' (Plut., *Ages.* 36.5).

Of course, there was no particular military uniform in an age when men went to war in their working clothes. The Spartan warrior probably wore the standard tunic (*chiton*) of the Greeks, often arranged to leave one shoulder bare, as when Kleomenes is described 'putting on his *chiton* and loosening the seam from his right shoulder' (Plut., *Kleom.* 37.2). Otherwise, there was a specifically one-armed tunic called an *exomis*, which the Byzantine lexicon known as the *Suda* defines as 'a *chiton* with only one arm-hole' (*Suda* E, 3290).

Although there was no uniform, the Spartans seem to have preferred one colour above all others. Xenophon records that, 'amongst the equipment for battle, Lykourgos arranged that they should have a red garment, believing it to be most fit for war while least resembling women's clothing' (Xen., *Lak. pol.* 11.3). Plutarch explains that, 'in warfare, they wear red garments, partly because it seems to be a manly colour, and partly because the bloody hue causes more terror amongst inexperienced foes; also, if a man has been wounded, it is not easily detected by the enemy but goes unnoticed because of the fortuitous similarity in colour' (Plut., *Inst. Lac.* 24 = *Mor.* 238F).

The last of these reasons is often the first to be emphasized by modern commentators, perhaps unduly influenced by the Roman writer Valerius Maximus, who believed that 'they used to wear scarlet tunics in battle to disguise and conceal the blood from their wounds, not because the sight of the wounds alarmed them, but in order not to build the enemy's confidence' (Val. Max. 2.6.2).

Plutarch represented 'the staff and the cloak' of Gylippos as the symbols of the Spartan warrior, specifically the Spartan officer. In 411 BC, the Spartan admiral (*nauarchos*) Astyochos was involved in a dispute with his sailors over pay which should have come from their new Persian paymasters; the admiral's surly attitude did nothing to calm the situation, but matters came to a head only when 'he brandished his staff (*bakteria*)' (Thuk. 8.84.2), whereupon the mob of sailors turned on him, forcing him to take refuge at an altar. Possibly, Astyochos considered it within his rights to beat a non Spartan as if he were a helot. If so, not every Spartan shared his opinion.

Around 404 BC, Lysander, as admiral of the fleet, is said to have rebuked the commander of the Spartan garrison in Athens, a certain Kallibios, for lifting his staff to strike the famous Athenian athlete Autolykos; Lysander accused him of 'not knowing how to govern free men' (Plut., *Lys*. 15.5), reinforcing the suggestion that beating with the *bakteria* was how Spartans governed helots.

Other Spartans are found using the *bakteria* to assert their authority; while in charge of a bridge-building detail of Greek mercenaries, for example, Klearchos 'carried a spear in his left hand and, in his right, his staff, and if he thought that any of those assigned to the task were shirking, he would pick out the right man and strike him' (Xen., *Anab*. 2.3.11). The two implements, spear and staff, are also found in the hands of Mnasippos, another Spartan admiral forced to deal with insubordination; when his men grumbled that they had not received their provisions, 'he beat one with his staff, and another with the spike-end of his spear' (Xen., *Hell*. 6.2.19).

EQUIPMENT

While on campaign, each Spartan warrior carried a spear (*dory*) and the distinctive circular shield (*aspis*) that was characteristic of hoplites. In addition, most wore a helmet of some kind, for head wounds were particularly debilitating, and a pair of greaves; and some may have worn a cuirass of some description, although Spartans often appear to have gone without.

The shield

The writer Diodorus Siculus refers to 'the men who were called hoplites because of their shields (*aspides*)' (Diod. 15.44.3), highlighting the fact that, without the *aspis*, the man was not a hoplite. More correctly, the hoplite was named after his *hopla*, a catch-all term for military gear, which naturally centred on the all-important shield, but could include helmet, greaves and weapons as well.

The remains of an Etruscan hoplite shield (the 'Bomarzo shield') in the Vatican's Museo Gregoriano Etrusco have enabled scholars to interpret its ingenious design. The core of the shield was a shallow wooden bowl whose

Tombstone of 'Lisas the Tegean', discovered at Dekeleia in 1873. As Spartan allies, Tegeans may have been garrisoned there from 413 BC. Lisas has adopted the Spartan warrior's *pilos* and *exomis*. (From *Bulletin de Correspondance Hellénique*, Vol. 4, 1880, pl. 7)

Scene from a red-figure amphora, depicting the departure of three bearded warriors. Inside the shield of the leftmost warrior, the spare *antilabe* can be seen. His companion holds his spear with both hands, suggesting that his shield has been slung on his back. (From E. Gerhard, *Auserlesene griechische Vasenbilder*, Vol. 4, Berlin, 1858, Tafel 26)

thickness varied between 10 and 11mm in the centre and 12 and 18mm at the edge. The exterior was faced with a sheet of bronze, only 0.5mm thick, which smoothly followed the shape of the shield and wrapped over the rim at the edge.

Inside the shield was the central armband (*porpax*), which took the form of a bronze sleeve designed to fit the hoplite's forearm snugly. To either side, a pair of staples were fastened to the shield's wooden core for attaching a braided cord handgrip (*antilabe*). Since the hoplite required only one handgrip, the provision of two pairs of staples was presumably to allow for a substitute; if the first one snapped, the shield could continue in use simply by rotating it through 180 degrees. Xenophon talks about a shield being *eurhythmos* or 'well-fitted' (Xen., *Mem.* 3.10.12), which presumably occurred when a man could grasp the *antilabe* in his fist, while up to his elbow in the *porpax*.

B THE SPARTAN SHIELD

The fortuitous survival of the so-called 'Bomarzo shield', now in the Museo Gregoriano Etrusco (Vatican), allows us to see how a hoplite shield (*aspis*) might have been assembled. The core of the shield was a shallow wooden bowl with a flat, projecting rim, constructed from several planks of poplar wood, arranged so that the grain ran horizontally when the shield was in use (**1**). The thickness seems to have varied between 10 and 11mm in the centre and 12 and 18mm at the edge.

A thin layer of leather was glued to the interior, while on the exterior, and perhaps stuck to it with a layer of pitch, was a bronze facing, 0.5mm thick. Around the rim, the bronze was often decorated with a repoussé pattern, such as the guilloche shown here (**2**). The classic Spartan shield of the late 5th century BC was probably blank and polished to a high sheen. However, vase paintings depict various shield emblems, including the snake shown here (**3**), and the pattern of radiating black and white crescents on a red background is thought to have had particular significance at Sparta (**4**). Some of the motifs carved on ivory votive disks from the Temple of Artemis Orthia are also found as shield emblems, such as the scorpion shown here (**5**). Equally, it has been suggested that bronze 'Medusa' plaques were intended to be attached to shields (**6**).

Inside the shield was the central armband (*porpax*) and, to either side, a pair of staples for attaching a braided cord handgrip (*antilabe*) (**7**). Vase paintings show how four additional anchor points allowed spare cord to be threaded around the perimeter, perhaps to assist in carrying the shield over the shoulder.

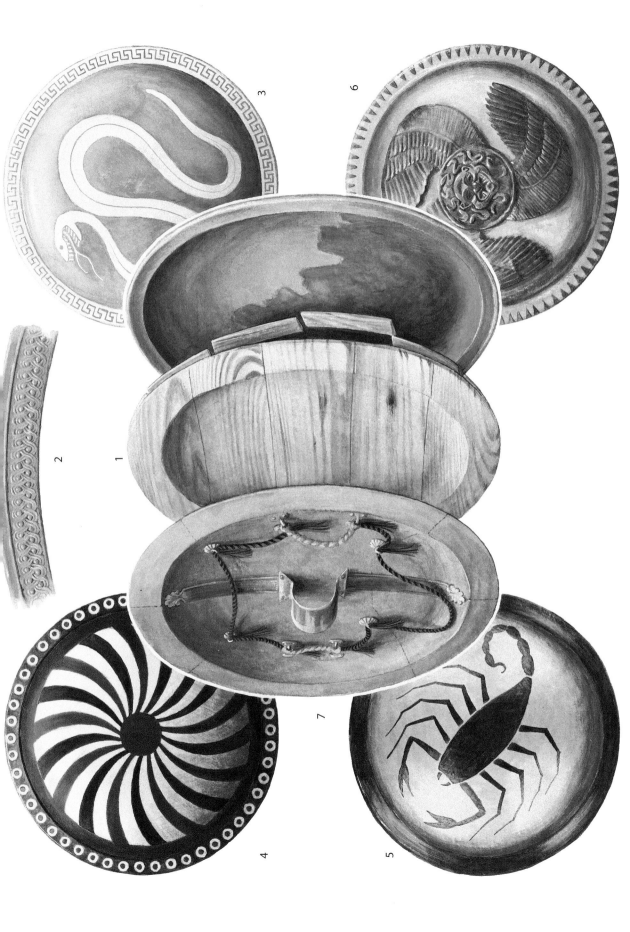

The weight of the Bomarzo shield, when new, has been estimated at a surprisingly manageable 6.5kg. The thin bronze facing contributed little to the shield's defensive value and, particularly when polished to a high sheen, probably had more of an aesthetic purpose. Certainly, Xenophon believed that the Spartans faced their shields with bronze 'because it was quickly polished and tarnished very slowly' (Xen., *Lak. pol.* 11.3).

The timber core ensured that the shield was effective against sword cuts, but it seems to have been vulnerable to determined spear thrusts. The Spartan general Brasidas, for example, was wounded by a spear through his shield; when asked how this had happened, he gave the laconic reply, 'my shield betrayed me' (Plut., *Ap. Lak.*, *Bras.* 2 = *Mor.* 219c). Earlier, during the Spartan amphibious attack on the Athenian position at Pylos in 425 BC, it was the shape and relative lightness of Brasidas' shield that carried it ashore when it was accidentally dropped in the water.

A genuine Spartan shield-facing was discovered during the 1936 excavations in the Athenian agora; it is slightly oval, measuring 95 x 83cm, with a smooth face and an elaborate guilloche ornamentation around the rim. Allowing for damage and distortion, this bronze facing must originally have belonged to a wooden shield slightly larger than the Bomarzo example. When originally displayed as booty on the walls of the Stoa Poikile, the shield would have been complete, for Aristophanes claimed that each still had its *porpax* (Ar., *Hipp.* 843–59), which was, of course, attached to the wooden core.

The characters in Aristophanes' play *Hippeis* are understandably alarmed at the prospect of battle-ready shields on public display in Athens, where they could easily be used by insurgents, for the spoils of war were normally

Bronze shield-facing, reconstructed from fragments discovered during excavations in the Athenian agora in 1936. The shield has an elaborately ornamented rim and carries a dedicatory inscription punched into the face, identifying it as one of those captured from the Spartans on Sphakteria in 425 BC. (Now in the Agora Museum, Athens. Photo © Stefanos Skarmintzos)

'neutralized'. Indeed, one ancient author tells us that, even in Sparta, 'the Spartiate removes the *porpax* from his *aspis* when he is at home, because of his mistrust of the helots' (Critias Frg. 37).

Enemies put to flight often discarded their shields in order to run away faster. But at Sparta, a warrior could commit few crimes worse than this, 'for the shield is intended for the common good of the battle-line' (Plut., *Ap. Lak.*, *Dem.* 2 = *Mor.* 220A). Clearly, if a hoplite discarded his shield, he jeopardized the safety of his comrades, for the *aspides* formed the shield-wall of the phalanx. On Sphakteria in 425 BC, the Spartans were at a disadvantage in their skirmish with the lightly armed Athenians, owing to the fact that they 'could not pursue them as they were carrying *hopla*' (Thuk. 4.33.2, where the *hopla* are clearly the hoplite shields).

Plato was keen to draw a distinction between a genuine *rhipsaspis* ('shield discarder') and a man who has simply lost his equipment by accident:

> How many have lost weapons (*hopla*) because of being thrown down from the cliffs, or at sea, or struggling in a storm when a sudden rush of water takes them by surprise… But if a man is surprised by the enemy and, instead of turning round and defending himself with the weapons (*hopla*) he has, he intentionally lets them drop or throws them away, preferring the coward's life of shame to the brave man's glorious and fortunate death, then there should certainly be a penalty for throwing weapons away like this. But if it was in the way that I described earlier, the judge must not fail to take the facts into consideration. (Pl., *Leg.* 944B–D)

The Spartans did not consider 'shield discarding' to be a laughing matter. The poet Archilochos was allegedly denied hospitality at Sparta for having written these flippant lines: 'some Thracian now struts around with my shield, blameless equipment which I was forced to toss into a thicket, but I myself escaped Death's clutches. Begone, shield! I shall get another one' (Plut., *Inst. Lac.* 34 = *Mor.* 239B). According to the *Suda*: 'Because of Lykourgos' laws, when mothers sent forth their sons to the wars, they used to say, referring to their shields, "Either this or on this", which means "Either bring this when you return, and don't be a shield-discarder (*rhipsaspis*), or be brought upon this as a corpse".' (*Suda* L, 824)

The same laconic phrase, 'Either this or on this', is repeated by several authors, one of whom claims that Aristotle had attributed the remark to Gorgo, wife of King Leonidas; but it is rather puzzling, as Spartan warriors were traditionally buried where they fell. Plutarch preserves the story as an anonymous one, along with a variation in which 'another woman, as her son went off to war, handed over his shield and said, "Your father always kept this safe for you; so should you also keep it safe, or stop living"' (Plut., *Lak. Ap., Anon.* 17 = *Mor.* 241F). Clearly, for a Spartan warrior, it was deeply shameful to lose a shield.

When in storage, the shield could be protected by a kind of dust cover called a *sagma*. The late Roman lexicographer Hesychius defines this item as 'the covering for an *aspis*'. Again, the *Suda* attempts a lengthier explanation:

> Aristophanes, in his play *Acharnians*, writes: 'Who woke the Gorgon from her covering?' For the Gorgon was portrayed on the shield (*aspis*); so he is saying, 'Who took the shield (*hoplon*, this time) out of its cover (*sagma*)?' (*Suda* S, 23; quoting Ar., *Acharn.* 574)

Scene from a red-figure *kylix*, depicting *ephebes* equipping themselves for war. The youth on the left is taking his shield from its dust cover (*sagma*). (From E. Gerhard, *Auserlesene griechische Vasenbilder*, Vol. 4, Berlin, 1858, Tafel 29)

It is unlikely that the cover was taken on campaign, because the shield had to be ever-ready. Ancient depictions demonstrate that it could be slung onto the back while on the march. A passage from Xenophon's *Anabasis* seems to describe this, when, in order to persuade his men to traverse a deep ravine, he offers them two courses

Terracotta relief from Apollonia Pontica, Thrace. The hoplite on the left carries his shield slung on his back while he blows a horn. (Now in the Louvre, Paris. Wikimedia Commons/ Marie-Lan Nguyen)

of action: 'Go forward with weapons (*hopla*) held out in front, or, with them slung behind, risk the enemy coming up behind us' (Xen., *Anab*. 6.5.16). Some have suggested that it was for this purpose that a cord was often pinned around the inside perimeter of the shield; others have seen this cord as spare material from which an emergency handgrip could be fashioned.

Shield emblems (*episema*)

It is well known that hoplite shields often carried painted designs or bronze appliqué blazons; one example is the Gorgoneion (or Medusa mask) in Aristophanes' *Acharnians* (quoted above). The philo-Spartan Alkibiades allegedly depicted Eros with a thunderbolt on his shield, which was thought to be far too frivolous (Plut., *Alk*. 16.2), whereas the Thebans depicted Herakles' club on theirs (Xen., *Hell*. 7.5.20). Plutarch even records the case of a Spartan who painted a life-sized fly on his shield, explaining that 'I move in so close to the enemy that the emblem is seen by them as big as it really is' (Plut., *Ap. Lak.*, *Anon*. 41 = *Mor*. 234C–D).

At one point, Xenophon describes how an Argive force identified its enemy as Sikyonians, 'seeing the *sigma* on their shields' (Xen., *Hell*. 4.4.10); clearly, on this occasion, the men of Sikyon had painted Σ on their shields, being the initial letter of their town. Similarly, modern writers often state as a fact that Spartan shields carried the Λ, indicating 'Lakedaimon'. However, the evidence is problematic.

Selection of lead figurines excavated at the Menelaion (Temple of Menelaos) at Sparta in 1909. The warriors' shields show a marked preference for the 'spoked wheel' pattern, prompting the excavators to comment on the absence of the expected Λ (*lambda*) symbol, thought to signify Lakedaimon. (Now in Sparta Museum. From *Annual of the British School at Athens*, Vol. 15, 1908–09)

Bronze plate (restored) representing a Gorgoneion, or face of Medusa, discovered in 1924 at the Temple of Athena Chalkioikos in Sparta. It is thought to be a shield emblem, dating from around 520 BC. (Now in the National Archaeological Museum, Athens. Photo © Stefanos Skarmintzos)

No contemporary source ever mentions this Spartan shield blazon, nor is it illustrated on any vase paintings, which provide the greatest source of evidence for these emblems. In fact, it is only the word of a Byzantine lexicographer named Photius, who wrote in his *Lexicon*, in the section on words beginning with L, under the heading '*Lambda*': 'the Lakedaimonians inscribed this on their shields, just like the Messenians and *Mu*. Eupolis writes: "I was terror-struck seeing the gleaming *lambda*"; thus also Theopompos'. So it seems that Photius had gleaned this snippet of information from the 4th-century BC historian Theopompos (whose work is now lost, but who appears to link the elusive Spartan Λ with a similarly unknown Messenian M). He, in turn, seems to have quoted a line from the Athenian comic poet Eupolis (whose work is also largely lost).

It is true that the Roman writer Pausanias, referring to a situation in the late 4th or early 3rd century BC (beyond the period covered here), claims that some Messenians treacherously infiltrated Elis 'with Lakonian emblems on their shields' (Paus. 4.28.5), but that is not the same as saying either that the Spartan shields carried a *lambda* emblem, or that the Messenians usually used a *Mu* emblem.

However, if we can trust that Theopompos really quoted a line from Eupolis, his testimony would relate squarely to the period of the Peloponnesian War, when that particular comic poet flourished. Indeed, one modern commentator has gone so far as to link the quotation with Kleon's defeat and death at Amphipolis, but this is pure speculation. Another commentator has suggested that the phrase should not be taken literally; on the contrary, it might conceal a vulgar joke of the kind beloved in Athenian

comedy, playing on the obscene verb *laikazein*, best translated by the Anglo-Saxon to 'f— off'. We could then imagine the unknown speaker in Eupolis' play interpreting the blank bronze shields of the Spartans as a dismissive message of this kind.

The spear

Every Greek hoplite's main weapon was the spear (*dory*). The cardinal importance of this weapon is highlighted by the fact that, according to the *Suda*, exemption from military service was known as *adoratia*, meaning literally 'spearlessness' (*Suda* A, 506). It was, quite naturally, the spear that first occurred to the poet Tyrtaios, when he encouraged every Spartan to fight well, with the words 'in his right hand let him brandish his mighty spear, let him shake the fearsome crest upon his head' (Tyrt. Frg. 11, lines 25–26).

Judging by their depiction in vase paintings, hoplite spears were at least one-and-a-third times the height of a man, or approximately 2.4m. Cornel wood and ash are thought to have been the preferred materials for the shaft (*kamax*). The head, known as the *akoke* or the *epidoratis* (literally, 'on top of the spear'), was usually made of iron, socketed and riveted to the shaft. The butt end, or *ouriachos* (from *oura*, meaning a 'tail'), was routinely fitted with a bronze spike known as a *styrax*, or more graphically as a *sauroter*

Scene from a black-figure *hydria* (water jar), *c.*575–525 BC, depicting hoplites fighting over a corpse. The men wear only helmets and greaves, and the visible shield-facings carry no emblems. The bronze-faced Spartan shields may have resembled these. (Now in the Louvre, Paris. Wikimedia Commons/Photo: Marie-Lan Nguyen)

Iron spearhead from Athens. Although the butt-spike was normally made of bronze, iron was preferred for the spearhead, because it could maintain a sharper edge. (Now in the National Archaeological Museum, Athens. Photo © Stefanos Skarmintzos)

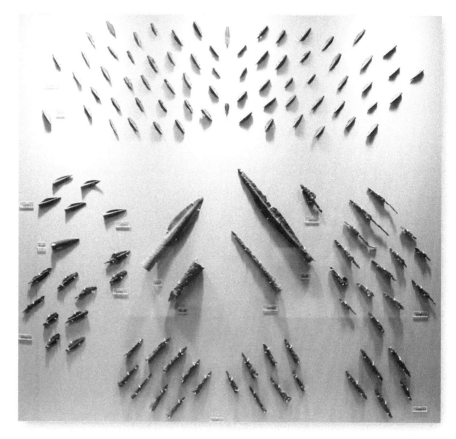

Selection of arrowheads, spearheads and a butt-spike collected during excavation work at Thermopylai in 1939. The arrowheads are likely to be Persian, but the spearheads and butt-spike probably belonged to King Leonidas' 300 Spartans. (Now in the National Archaeological Museum, Athens. Photo © Livius.org)

Two bronze inscribed spear-butts from Olympia. The inscription, *Methanioi apo Lakedaimonion*, indicates that the Messenians (in their local spelling) dedicated a spear taken 'from the Spartans', perhaps at Stenykleros. The inscription covers three sides with the message 'Theodoros dedicates this to the King'. (From *Journal of Hellenic Studies*, Vol. 2, 1881, pl. 11)

('lizard-sticker'). Insubordinate soldiers struck by the *styrax* of their officer's spear would not soon forget it.

The butt-spike enabled the hoplite to ground his spear when it wasn't immediately required. Diodorus Siculus describes the mercenary hoplites of Chabrias, awaiting a Spartan attack by Agesilaos' troops in 378 BC, 'with their shields leaning against their knee and their spears upright'

Selection of assorted spear-butts (*styrakes* or *sauroteres*) dedicated to Athena on the Akropolis at Athens. No. 6844 (second down) has *Athenaias* ('of Athena') punched along the side. (Now in the National Archaeological Museum, Athens. Photo © Stefanos Skarmintzos)

(Diod. 15.32.5). This was the hoplite's stance when 'at ease'; the Greek word for a lull in the fighting, *anakokes*, was supposed to derive from this habit of holding the spear point (*akoke*) upright (*ana*) (*Suda* A, 1914).

On campaign, the Spartan warrior kept his spear with him at all times. Xenophon claims that the reason for this was the same as for keeping the helots away from where the arms were stored in the camp (Xen., *Lak. pol.* 12.4), namely that the helot servants were not to be trusted. (As we have seen, Spartan shields, when at home, were allegedly disabled for the same reason.)

The sword

Hoplites often carried a sword as a sidearm, but rather than the curved sabre (*machaira*) depicted in many vase paintings, the Spartans favoured the straight or leaf-shaped blade (*xiphos*). In addition, the swords of the Spartans were famously shorter than the thigh-length blades used by other Greeks. The Athenian Demades sneered at this, saying that 'conjurors swallow Spartan swords because they are so short', but the Spartan King Agis III

Scene from a red-figure *kylix* signed by the painter Douris (*c*.490–460 BC), depicting the legendary Spartan King Menelaos pursuing the Trojan prince Paris. Menelaos carries the short, straight sword favoured by the Spartans. (Now in the Louvre, Paris. Wikimedia Commons/Marie-Lan Nguyen)

replied (with characteristic brevity), 'quite so, but the Spartans can still reach their enemies with them' (Plut., *Ap. Lak.*, *Agis* 1 = *Mor.* 216C).

The Spartan sword was technically known as an *encheiridion*, meaning 'little hand weapon'. This is the word used by the Spartan admiral Antalkidas, when he explained why the Spartan short sword was so effective: 'the reason is that we fight close up to the enemy' (Plut., *Ap. Lak.*, *Ant.* 8 = *Mor.* 217E). Indeed, when one Spartan lad complained about the size of his sword, his mother simply replied, 'then add a stride' (Plut., *Lak. Ap.*, *Anon.* 18 = *Mor.* 241F).

The short sword should not be confused with the curved Spartan knife (*xyele*), useful for whittling. Xenophon knew a Spartan named Drakontios, who had been exiled since boyhood for accidentally killing another boy with a blow from his *xyele* (Xen., *Anab.* 4.8.25). Plutarch even records an instance of such a knife fight, after which the wounded boy begged his friends not to avenge him, 'because I would have done the same, if only I had been skilful and had acted first' (Plut., *Ap. Lak.*, *Anon.* 34 = *Mor.* 233F).

The helmet

The iconic Spartan helmet (*kranos*) was the so-called 'Corinthian', which concealed the entire face apart from the eyes and mouth. This is the style of helmet most commonly depicted on the early Spartan bronze statuettes, and can also be seen amongst the locally manufactured lead figurines deposited in the sanctuary of Artemis Orthia and in the Menelaion.

The helmet was skilfully beaten out of bronze, and early examples dating broadly to the 7th century BC have stitch-holes punched around the edge for attaching a fabric lining. By the 6th century BC, a more elegant version had appeared, whose streamlined shape brought its weight down to around

1kg. The absence of stitch-holes may indicate that a fabric lining was glued in place, but a padded felt cap could simply have been worn underneath. Such padding was required, not only to make the helmet more comfortable, but also (perhaps more importantly) to cushion blows to the head.

The famous marble sculpture of a warrior from Sparta demonstrates that a crest could be worn, though the method of fixing it to the helmet is unknown. The crests illustrated on vase paintings were probably of dyed horsehair, but an exchange between the characters in Aristophanes' *Acharnians*, one of whom says 'Now give me the plumage from your helmet' (Ar., *Acharn.* 584), shows that feathers were often used.

The Corinthian style of helmet must have been very stuffy and claustrophobic in the heat of a Peloponnesian summer; many hoplites seem to have worn a headband, probably to prevent perspiration from running into their eyes. When at ease, the wearer could certainly push the helmet back from his face, but this was not practicable in battle. Even if the wearer was willing to forego the helmet's facial protection, when pushed back, it could easily be knocked from his head.

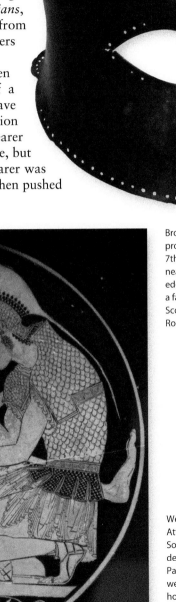

Bronze Corinthian helmet, probably dating from the later 7th century BC. The rivet-holes neatly punched around the edges could be for attaching a fabric lining. (From the J. L. Scott collection, Glasgow. © Ross H. Cowan)

Well-known scene from an Attic red-figure *kylix* by the Sosias Painter, *c.*500 BC, depicting Achilles binding Patroklos' wound. Patroklos wears a cap of the sort which hoplites may have worn beneath their helmets. (Now in the Altes Museum, Berlin. Wikimedia Commons/Bibi Saint-Pol)

Spartan black-figure *kylix*, c.550 BC, depicting the hero Kadmos fighting the Theban dragon. The Gorgoneion emblem appears on his shield. (Now in the Louvre, Paris. Wikimedia Commons/Bibi Saint-Pol)

Consequently, a new style of helmet appeared, based on the conical brimless cap known as a *pilos*. In fact, the Roman philosopher Pollux equated the '*pilos* and *encheiridion*' with Sparta (Poll. 1.149). In its original form, the *pilos* was a felt cap worn by workmen and travellers, and was particularly associated with the Peloponnese; the word literally refers to the method of 'compressing' wool to make felt.

RIGHT
Bronze plaque, thought to be the cheek-piece of a helmet, discovered at the ancient shrine of Dodona. The main figure wears a *pilos* helmet and carries the hoplite shield. (Now in the National Archaeological Museum, Athens. Photo © Stefanos Skarmintzos)

FAR RIGHT
Bronze *pilos* helmet with assorted arrowheads. (Now in the War Museum, Athens. Photo © Stefanos Skarmintzos)

Some scholars have suggested that this felt hat was simply worn as a liner underneath a Corinthian-style helmet, but its conical shape would be a poor fit. Others have suggested that Spartan hoplites had exchanged their bronze helmets for felt caps, but many bronze helmets shaped like *piloi* have been found.

A reading of Thukydides' *History* suggests that, by 425 BC, the *pilos* had become the standard headgear of the Spartan warrior; in that year, the men trapped on Sphakteria found that 'their *piloi* would not fend off the arrows' of the Athenian archers, 'and javelins broke on striking' (Thuk. 4.34.3). Some scholars have taken this to mean that the Spartans were wearing the conical felt cap, which would not have been proof against arrows, but Thukydides is probably drawing attention to the fact that the *pilos*, when compared with the Corinthian, leaves a larger area of the head exposed. Furthermore, only a bronze helmet would break javelins, so it seems that the Spartans were, by now, wearing the bronze *pilos*.

The cuirass

At the beginning of our period, many Spartan warriors will have worn the bronze 'bell cuirass' (*thorax*), in which a front plate and a back plate, both covering from neck to waist, were fastened together. This is the style worn by archaic Spartan bronze figurines, such as the well-known example from Dodona. The design resembles a bell by gently flaring inwards at the waist before jutting out in a flange, which was no doubt intended to catch or deflect any downward spear thrusts.

It is possible that the Spartan warrior, following the example set by the hoplites of other city-states, graduated, along with them, from the cumbersome bronze bell cuirass to the more comfortable fabric corslet. Xenophon describes this *thorax lineos* ('linen corslet'), which covered a man down to his abdomen and incorporated a skirt of fabric strips called *pteryges* (Xen., *Anab.* 4.7.15). This design of corslet, with its telltale shoulder flaps, is frequently depicted on vase paintings, but is nowhere explicitly linked with Spartans.

The bronze 'bell' cuirass and associated helmet discovered in 1953 in a late 8th-century grave. The cuirass appeared to have been lined with cloth. The helmet, of 'Kegelhelm' type, is a forerunner of the Illyrian style, which lacks the characteristic nasal guard of the Corinthian style. (Now in Argos Museum. Photo © Sarah C. Murray)

Scene from a black-figure *krater*, *c.*575–550 BC, depicting hoplites fighting over the corpse of Hippolytos. The men wear the archaic panoply and carry the large hoplite shield, one of which displays the popular Gorgoneion motif. (Now in the Louvre, Paris. Wikimedia Commons/ Marie-Lan Nguyen)

The death of the Spartan mercenary Kleonymos in 401 BC demonstrates that there was an alternative to the fabric corslet, for Xenophon records how he was 'shot in the side by an arrow that penetrated his shield and *spolas*' (Xen., *Anab.* 4.1.18). The late Roman lexicographer Hesychius gives a straightforward definition of this garment as 'a short, thick *chiton* made of leather, being the leather corslet'. Unfortunately, it is unclear how we would recognize such a garment, if it were depicted in a vase painting.

Besides the obvious practicality of wearing some form of body protection, Plutarch tells the story of the *hebon* named Isidas who was fined for fighting 'bare without *hopla* or *himation*' (Plut., *Ages.* 34.7), while heroically defending Sparta in 362 BC. However, in this instance, the *hopla* need not include a corslet; Plutarch's story may simply indicate that Isidas lacked a helmet and, especially, a shield, for he is described 'holding a javelin in one hand and a sword in the other'.

Equally, when Xenophon says that Agesilaos 'armed his men so that it seemed as if they were all bronze and all crimson' (Xen., *Ages.* 2.7), he is probably drawing attention to the bronze helmets and shields. Nor is there any mention of corslets amongst Xenophon's troops in mercenary service in Persia: 'all had bronze helmets, crimson tunics, and greaves, and had uncovered shields' (Xen., *Anab.* 1.2.16). In fact, it seems to have been quite permissible to discard helmet and corslet, on the grounds that these items

C SPARTAN WARRIOR, c.346 BC

By the time of the Third Sacred War, Sparta had passed her heyday; her army was overwhelmingly Lakedaimonian, rather than Spartiate. Consequently, the Spartan Warrior played a far smaller role on the battlefield. Nor is it clear, in the absence of archaeological finds and literary descriptions, what type of armour he wore.

During the period of the Peloponnesian War, there seems to have been a deliberate lightening of equipment. The claustrophobic 'Corinthian' helmet was replaced by the *pilos* (**1**), which left the face, ears and neck exposed. Although this was a far simpler helmet, several examples are known to have been decorated with repoussé or appliqué work, and a bronze statuette (now in Sparta Museum) shows how a crest could be applied. At the same time, the bronze cuirass and greaves, which had been worn during the time of the Persian Wars, were given up entirely. The Spartiates on Sphakteria, for example, relied only on the protection of their shields (**2**). Much the same state of affairs probably continued into the 4th century BC, as long as the dwindling population of Spartiates clung to their heroic traditions.

By contrast, the hoplites of other city-states had given up the bronze cuirass in favour of the lightweight fabric corslet, still designated as a *thorax* (**3**); this incorporated a tubular body section (as opposed to the front- and back-plates of the cuirass) and a collar or 'yoke' section, to which the body 'tube' was attached (hence, the common neologism, 'tube-and-yoke corslet'). Although the fabric seems often to have been quilted or even reinforced with metal scales, it did not offer complete protection. At the Second battle of Mantineia, when Epameinondas, the victor of Leuktra, 'took a blow to the *thorax*, he fell on the spot, for the spear had broken leaving the iron point in his body' (Diod. 15.87.1).

Hoplites wishing more protection than the *pilos* could offer, but unwilling to suffer the discomfort of the 'Corinthian' helmet, often elected to wear the more open-faced helmet known to scholars as the 'Chalcidian'. Variations included the removal of the nose guard and the attachment of hinged cheek-pieces, often shown folded up on vase paintings (**4**).

The same paintings show that greaves might still be worn, at the individual's discretion. But, as before, the warrior's main protection came from the large hoplite shield (*aspis*), here shown depicting the cockerel, a belligerent bird that was sacred to Herakles and, no doubt for that reason, a popular Spartan motif (**5**). It is possible that the *perioikoi* who increasingly filled out the ranks of the Lakedaimonian army wore equipment like this.

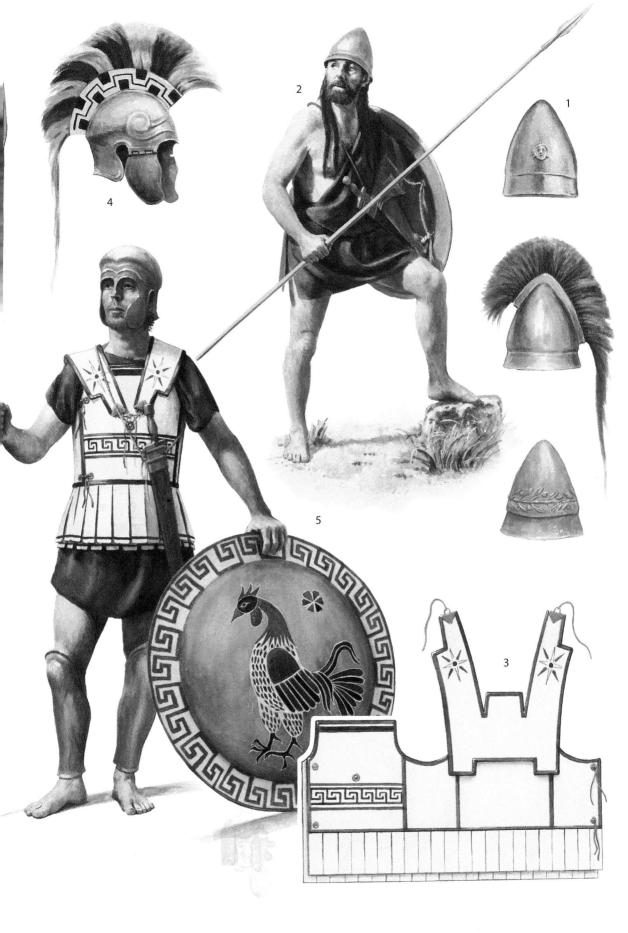

Scene from a black-figure amphora, *c.*560–540 BC, depicting a warrior arming for battle. He wears his Corinthian helmet pushed back from his face, while putting on a pair of greaves. (Now in the Louvre, Paris. Wikimedia Commons/ Bibi Saint-Pol)

were worn by personal preference, and it was probably Isidas' lack of a shield – normally a serious offence at Sparta – that led to his fine.

Greaves

The evidence for Spartan greaves (*knemides*) is as equivocal as the evidence for corslets; both items appear on the archaic bronze figurines, but there is little evidence thereafter. However, where the hoplite shield might mitigate the absence of body armour, it seldom covered a man's lower legs, where greaves would provide the only protection.

If the Spartan elected to wear greaves, each bronze *knemis* must have been modelled, albeit roughly, to fit his leg, because it wrapped around the shin leaving only a narrow gap at the back, along the wearer's calf. The springiness of the bronze kept the greaves in place and, as with the helmet, padding provided comfort while cushioning any blows.

We can assume that such padding was normally made of fabric, but Aristotle claims that marine sponges could be used, and particularly the species nicknamed 'the sponge of Achilles': 'this one they place under the helmet and greaves, to deaden the sound of the blow' (Arist., *Hist. An.* 5.14 = 548B). Of course, in deadening the sound, it also absorbed the impact, which was surely its primary purpose.

MILITARY SERVICE

Every Spartiate between the ages of 20 and 59 was liable for military service. No ancient author tells us this directly, but we have seen that the *hebontes* always formed part of the army, and it seems that, once a man became a *geron* (elder), he was excused from the call-up.

Xenophon states that one of the responsibilities of the ephors was to 'announce the "years" which are required to take the field' (Xen., *Lak. pol.* 11.2); in practice, it seems that the Spartans were classified by age-group, spanning ten years. In 371 BC, for example, when the ephors mobilized the army, they went 'as far as the 40 from youth' (Xen., *Hell.* 6.4.17). Just as the *hebontes* were the 'ten from youth', men aged 50–59 were the '40 from youth', so on this occasion the ephors had effectively called up every man between the ages of 20 and 59.

In 378 BC, King Agesilaos refused the field command against Thebes, on the grounds that 'others of his age were no longer obliged to serve outside their homeland' (Xen., *Hell.* 5.4.13). However, it is not Agesilaos' age that is the issue here, for, by then, he was probably 66 years old; rather, it is the fact that he specifically includes himself amongst those who were 'over 40 from youth'. So we can be sure that those aged 60 and over (the *gerontes*, in fact) were usually excused military service.

Mess-groups (*syssitia*)

The basic grouping of Spartan warriors was the *syssition* ('mess-group') of around 15 *homoioi*; the precise number, if there was one, is not known,

but Plutarch claims that 'they met in fifteens, some fewer or more' (Plut., *Lyk*. 12.2). The *hebontes*, although not yet adults in many respects, appear to have qualified for membership. However, as with the *hippeis*, there was an element of selection.

Firstly, there was the self-selection, by which membership was limited to those Spartans who could contribute the required amount of food each month from their *kleros*, or plot of land. Plutarch claims that this comprised 'one *medimnos* of barley, eight *choes* of wine, five *minai* of cheese, and five half-*minai* of figs' (Plut., *Lyk*. 12.2; see glossary for these measures). Aristotle was critical of this contributory system, on the grounds that 'it is not at all democratic when it is regulated in this manner, for it is not easy for the very poor to participate' (Arist., *Pol*. 2.9 = 1271A).

Although Plato maintained that the *syssitia* had been invented for warfare (Pl., *Leg*. 633A) – and this certainly rings true, as it appears as a synonym for *syskenia*, or 'tent groups' (e.g. Xen., *Lak. pol*. 5.2) – there was also a tradition that Lykourgos had introduced the mess-groups as a levelling measure, 'so that the rich man may have no advantage over the poor man' (Plut., *Ap. Lak*., *Lyk*. 4 = *Mor*. 226E; and cf. Xen., *Lak. pol*. 7.3). Nevertheless, as Aristotle realized, there were inevitably those whose *kleros* could not support the required level of contributions.

There was a second level of selection, as each Spartan who qualified for entry still had to find a mess-group willing to have him. Each *hebon* seems to have made an application to a particular *syssition* of his choice; Plutarch describes how the current members voted on his acceptance by casting morsels of bread into an urn, with a single negative vote meaning that he was rejected.

The *syssition*, being a 'mess-group', was, of course, all about dining. Even beyond the age of 60, *gerontes* seem still to have taken their main meal in the *syssition*. The philosopher Dikaiarchos, one of Aristotle's pupils and the author of a lost *Spartan Constitution*, gave a full description of 'the meal eaten by the *syssitia*' in another lost work, entitled *Tripolitikon*; fortunately, the relevant passage was preserved by the Roman writer Athenaeus:

> The dinner is at first served separately to each man, and there is no sharing with one another. Afterwards there is a barley-cake, as large as each man desires, and a cup is set beside him, for drinking whenever he wishes. The same food, namely a piece of boiled pork, is always given to everyone; sometimes, however, they have nothing but a small bit of meat weighing as little as a quarter portion. Besides this, there is nothing else except, of course, the broth made from it, sufficient to go round all of them throughout the whole dinner; there may possibly be an olive or cheese or a fig, or they may even get something contributed specially, like a fish, a hare, or a pigeon, or some such thing. Afterwards, having hastily finished their dinner, these so-called *epaikla* ('additions') are passed around. Each man contributes to the mess-group (per month) about three Attic half-*medimnoi* of barley and eleven or twelve *choes* of wine, and besides this, a certain weight of cheese and figs, and furthermore, for purchasing food, about ten Aiginetan *obols*. (Athen., *Deipn.* 4.19 = 141B–C)

Ivory relief of a warship, discovered in 1907 in the Sanctuary of Artemis Orthia at Sparta. On the right, a warrior crouches on the prow; above him, a man is fishing. On the left, the personification of Artemis waves farewell. Ivory was a rare and expensive commodity in Greece. Now in the National Archaeological Museum, Athens. (Photo © Stefanos Skarmintzos)

The reference to 'ten Aiginetan *obols*' (the *obol* was the coin traditionally placed in the mouth of the deceased to pay the ferryman) jars with the notorious Spartan avoidance of coinage (at least until a later period), but the rest of Dikaiarchos' description rings true. His 'three Attic half-*medimnoi* of barley' are the equivalent of Plutarch's single Spartan *medimnos* (see glossary), and his '11 or 12 *choes* of wine' probably represent an attempt to translate Plutarch's eight Spartan *choes* into Attic measure. These amounts tally, in part, with the daily rations of 'two Attic *choinikes* of barley and two *kotylai* of wine and some meat' (Thuk. 4.16.1) sent to the Spartans trapped on Sphakteria in 425 BC; over the course of a 30-day month, these would have amounted to ⅚ *medimnos* of barley, but only 3⅓ *choes* of wine.

It has been observed that the monthly mess contributions far exceeded the amount that one man was likely to consume, and it may be that the *hebontes*, not being full adult Spartans, were excused their contribution. If so, this would have implications for the ownership of a *kleros*, which was perhaps only really required once a Spartan had turned 30 or had married. Nevertheless, even removing, say, five contributions from the total (for there can only have been four or five *hebontes* per *syssition* at any particular time) still leaves a surplus of food, and it is possible that each man's helot servant was expected to be fed also.

The main Spartan staple was the so-called black broth (*melas zomos*, elsewhere called *haimatia*, or 'blood-broth'), which the older men so enjoyed that they would even forego their piece of meat provided they had this soup. Although the ingredients are unknown, Plutarch elsewhere records that, in general, 'Spartans give the cook only vinegar and salt, and tell him to find the rest in the animal carcass' (Plut., *De san.* 12 = *Mor.* 128c). Even the Spartanized Alkibiades is represented 'nuzzling a barley-cake and devouring black broth' (Plut., *Alk.* 23.3). By contrast, and clearly for comedic effect, the Athenian comic poet Eupolis represents Alkibiades wishing for a frying pan (Athen., *Deipn.* 1.30 = 17d), the very antithesis of Spartan cooking!

Although the Spartans loved their black broth, they also appreciated occasional *epaikla* ('additions'); Xenophon notes that 'many extras were produced from hunting expeditions, and there were times when wealthy individuals contributed wheaten bread' (Xen., *Lak. pol.* 5.3). Other writers mention a snack called *kammatides*, consisting of barley soaked in oil and wrapped in laurel leaves.

Bronze warrior figurine from the sanctuary of Apollo Korythos near Koroni on the south-eastern coast of Messenia. His panoply has been supplemented by wrist- and thigh-guards. Now in the National Archaeological Museum, Athens. (Photo © Stefanos Skarmintzos)

The Spartan kings had their own *syssitia*, in which they were each joined by two Pythioi, the men whose job it was to consult the Delphic oracle. When on campaign, a Spartan king dined with the *polemarchoi* and 'three other men of the *homoioi*' (Xen., *Lak. pol.* 13.1), who looked after the provisions, while the others concentrated on the affairs of war. It is not clear whether a king resident at Sparta had the same dining companions, although Plutarch implies that King Agis, on his return from Mantineia in 418 BC, was supposed to dine with at least some of the *polemarchoi*, for it was they who refused to send his portion to his house, when he decided to dine with his wife (Plut., *Ap. Lak.*, *Lyk.* 6 = *Mor.* 226f–227a; *Lyk.* 12.3). At home, he would have been entitled to 'two *choinikes* of barley and a *kotyle* of wine' (Hdt. 6.57.3), but received a double portion in the *syssitia*, in case he wished to honour anyone by sharing his food.

The mess-groups were a forum for frank and informal political and philosophical discussion, helped along by free-flowing wine (perhaps as much as a litre per man every day), so it is not surprising that their maxim was 'Not a word goes out through these doors' (Plut., *Lyk.* 12.5; *Inst. Lac.* 1 = *Mor.* 236f). The membership comprised Spartiates of widely differing ages, from *hebontes* to *gerontes*, so it was true that, in this way, 'the younger might learn from the experience of those older' (Xen., *Lak. pol.* 5.5). Equally, the group was self-selecting, inasmuch as every member had been unanimously approved. So it seems unlikely (and entirely unworkable) for the membership of each *syssition* to be arranged – as some scholars have suggested – so that, when several (perhaps three) *syssitia* came together as an *enomotia*, every year from 20 up to 60 was represented.

Spartiate status was closely allied to the membership of a *syssition*, so those who were forced to withdraw also forfeited their status, becoming inferior to the *homoioi*. Such individuals were probably the *hypomeiones*, literally 'inferiors', whom Xenophon mentions (Xen., *Hell.* 3.3.6).

Army organization: the 'obal' army

The Spartan army of the Persian Wars (*c*.480 BC) is sometimes called the 'obal' army, because it was thought to have been based on units raised

Bronze sword acquired from the collection of T. B. Sandwith, British consul in Crete from 1870 until 1885. Although its provenance is unknown, it is often represented as Spartan, but this attribution seems unlikely. (Now in the British Museum, London. Photo © Stefanos Skarmintzos)

amongst the five *obai* or Spartan villages. Some scholars have tried to link these five villages with the five *lochoi* (regiments) listed by Aristotle in his lost *Spartan Constitution* (Frg. 541). These, according to a later 'scholiast', or ancient commentator, on Aristophanes' *Lysistrata*, were named *Edolos*, *Sinis*, *Arimas*, *Ploas*, and *Messoages*. (Hesychius explains that 'Aristophanes declares that there are four *lochoi* of the Lakedaimonians, yet there are five, as Aristotle says'.) However, only the last one, *Messoages*, bears even a passing resemblance to the name of a Spartan village, so the Oxford classicist Theodore Wade-Gery suggested that these were actually the regiments' nicknames

Indeed, Hans Van Wees has gone so far as to suggest that, at some early stage of development, the five *lochoi* of the 'obal' army were given warlike epithets evoking the Homeric world of epic poetry: *Edolos*, the 'Devourer'; *Sinis*, the 'Ravager'; *Arimas*, 'Hell-Bent' (from an adjective meaning 'furiously eager'); *Ploas*, the 'Thundercloud'; and *Messoages*, the 'Leader of the Centre' (which was the traditional position of the Spartan king in battle).

However, Herodotos has thrown this logical scheme into disorder with his mention of a *lochos Pitanates*, or 'Pitanate regiment', which was under the command of a certain Amompharetos at the battle of Plataia in 479 BC. It is difficult to escape the conclusion that this must have been a regiment raised by the village of Pitana. However, Thukydides denied that there had ever been a Pitanate *lochos*, 'for it did not ever exist' (Thuk. 1.20.3). Many ingenious theories have been hatched attempting to absolve Herodotos from blame, none more elegant than Van Wees' suggestion that Herodotos' source had used 'Pitana' to mean Sparta, a poetic metaphor used by Euripides amongst others. So, it seems likely that Thukydides was correct. (Had Herodotos' source simply told him that Amompharetos was 'commanding one of the Spartan *lochoi*'?)

Herodotos mentions the *syssitia* and the *enomotiai*, which remained the basic building blocks of the Spartan army, but the only officers he names are the *polemarchoi* and *taxiarchoi*. The first of these were the senior officers of the Spartan army, who could be assigned various responsibilities; in 480 BC, a *polemarchos* named Euainetos was entrusted with the advance guard

D

SPARTAN TACTICS

The writer Xenophon, a keen observer of Spartan affairs in the early 4th century BC, described how an army on the march formed up for battle. 'When they march in column', he writes, 'each *enomotia* naturally follows the tail of another *enomotia*; if, in such a situation, an enemy phalanx suddenly appears in front, the order is passed to each *enomotarches* to form up in line to the left, and so on down the entire column, until the phalanx is in position against the enemy' (Xen., *Lak. pol.* 11.8, using the phrase 'to the shield side' to mean 'to the left').

Xenophon explains that this is one of the easier manoeuvres, although he admits that the non-Spartan tacticians consider it to be tricky. In fact, the army of King Agis found itself in just such a situation at Mantineia in 418 BC, and 'they immediately and speedily formed up in line, Agis the King directing everything, according to the laws' (Thuk. 5.66.2).

At Mantineia, Thukydides explains that each *lochos* (the picture depicts a single *lochos*) consisted of four *pentekostyes* (shown bracketed in black), and each *pentekostys* consisted of four *enomotiai* (shown as a red square); furthermore, each *enomotia* drew up four men abreast and generally eight men deep. The individual officers were numbered amongst the men, meaning that the *lochagos* himself was also the *enomotarches* of the leading *enomotia* and the *pentekonter* of the leading four *enomotiai*. Our illustration depicts such a *lochos*, roughly 500 strong, forming up into a phalanx from its line of march, in the way that King Agis' army must have done. Each *enomotarches* is tagged with a red circle.

Lochagos

Entomarches

Bronze warrior figurine, wearing an early form of Corinthian helmet (it lacks a nose-guard and sports a spectacular crest fitting), along with a 'bell' cuirass and greaves. (Now in the National Archaeological Museum, Athens. Photo © Stefanos Skarmintzos)

against the invading Persians, and the Arimnestos who fell at Stenykleros in 464 BC may have been a *polemarchos*, too.

The *taxiarchos*, on the other hand, was Herodotos' version of the Spartan *lochagos*, a battlefield commander in charge of one of the five 1,000-strong *lochoi* into which the 'obal' army was divided. At Plataia in 479 BC, when the regent Pausanias ordered the retreat, all of the '*taxiarchoi*' (properly *lochagoi*) obeyed, except one: the dissenter was Amompharetos, whom (as we have seen) Herodotos believed to be the commander of the 'Pitanate regiment'; his four colleagues are not named. However, Herodotos' use of the Athenian term *taxiarchos* indicates that his source was not a Spartan one, and bolsters the case for his misunderstanding of the name of Amompharetos' regiment.

The army that Thukydides describes 50 or so years later was essentially the same, except for the fact that an additional tier of command had appeared. For Thukydides describes how 'the King gives orders to the *polemarchoi*, who convey them to the *lochagoi*, and they in turn to the *pentekonteres*, and they again to the *enomotarchoi*, and they to the *enomotia*' (Thuk. 5.66.3). Here are Herodotos' *polemarchoi* and *lochagoi* (masquerading as '*taxiarchoi*') along with the *enomotia* as the fundamental unit; but a *pentekonter* (a name that ought to mean 'commander of 50') has been added, leading Thukydides to observe (in an extravagant and obvious exaggeration) that 'almost all of the Lakedaimonian army are officers commanding other officers, except for a few, and the responsibility for action devolves upon many' (Thuk. 5.66.4). Unfortunately, the selection process for Spartan officers remains a mystery, but the constant competition from the age of seven perhaps created a natural hierarchy.

King Agis' deployment for the battle of Mantineia in 418 BC was based on the same five *lochoi* known to Aristotle, with the obvious addition, on the left wing, of a 600-strong *lochos* of Skiritai, specialist troops from Skiritis on the northern marches of Lakedaimon, and two *lochoi* of former helots (*neodamodeis*), including the Brasideioi (or 'men of Brasidas' who had fought under that general in Thrace in 424 BC). However, where 5,000 Spartiates had manned the five *lochoi* at Plataia, each *lochos* at Mantineia now consisted of only 500 men, a shocking confirmation of their declining population.

A band of brothers: the *enomotia*

The *enomotiai* were literally 'bound by oath'. An inscribed stele, found at Acharnai near Athens and dating from the time of the Persian Wars, seems to preserve the oath that the Spartiates swore:

> I shall fight while I live, and I shall not put life before being free, and I shall not desert my *taxiarchos* nor my *enomotarches*, whether he is alive or dead, and I shall not depart unless the leaders lead us away, and I shall do whatever the generals command, and I shall bury on the spot the dead among my fellow-fighters, and I shall leave no-one unburied. (Rhodes & Osborne, *Greek Historical Inscriptions*, §88, lines 23–31, modified)

The tenor of the oath, placing honour above life itself, is quite in tune with everything we know about the Spartan warrior. For example, the death of a Spartan king in battle brought horrific casualties amongst the Spartiates as they struggled to retrieve his body, 'for amongst the Lakedaimonians it was considered most shameful to allow the body of a king to come into the hands of the enemy' (Paus. 9.13.10). When he wrote these words, Pausanias was thinking about the death of Kleombrotos at Leuktra in 371 BC, but a similar scene had been enacted a century before, when King Leonidas fell at Thermopylai and his Spartiate comrades 'courageously dragged his corpse away, repulsing the enemy four times' (Hdt. 7.225.1).

Along with the *enomotiai*, Herodotos listed the *syssitia* as 'military institutions', so membership of a mess-group clearly bore some relationship to the mustering of the Spartan army. Equally, as Xenophon's word for the mess-group, *syskenia*, literally means a 'tent party', it is likely that each *enomotia* comprised men from a fixed number of *syssitia*. We have seen that each *syssition* numbered around 15 Spartiates; but, as the ephors announced which ten-year age-groups were required to take the field, it is unlikely that an entire *syssition* was ever mobilized (particularly as most included *gerontes*, and some of the *hebontes* may have been selected to serve seperately with the *hippeis*).

Thukydides' analysis of King Agis' army shows that 'in each *lochos* there were four *pentekostyes*, and in each *pentekostys* four *enomotiai*' (Thuk. 5.68.3), but the size of the *enomotia* continues to exercise scholars. The *Suda* claims that it was 'a military unit of 25 men used by the Lakedaimonians; derived from the oath-taking not to desert the unit' (*Suda* E , 1408); the derivation is certainly correct, but the size is far too small, at least for the period of Sparta's heyday. The fact that the detachment of Spartans occupying Sphakteria in 425 BC numbered 420 has suggested to some that it comprised 12 *enomotiai* of 35 men. On the other hand, 'there were 30-odd hoplites' (Thuk. 4.31.2) in the outpost subsequently surprised by the Athenian attackers, which might imply that there were actually 14 *enomotiai* of 30 men on the island.

At Mantineia in 418 BC, the *enomotiai* were drawn up in ranks of four and 'generally eight deep' (Thuk. 5.68.3), which ought to indicate an average of 32 men. Equally, a maximum of 36 men is implied at Leuktra in 371 BC, where each *enomotia* was drawn up in three files of 'no more than 12 men' (Xen., *Hell*. 6.4.12). The fluctuating sizes probably reflect the variable number of Spartiates who were liable for the call-up in any particular *syssition*. One thing seems certain: the scholars who presume that each *enomotia* contained one man from each year of every 'age-group' (say, from the ages of 20 up to 54, or even from 18 to 60!) have gone far beyond the evidence.

Finally, Herodotos' puzzling *triekas* ('30') continues to vex scholars, but the fact that it never appears in the pages of Thukydides or Xenophon may give us a clue to its original significance. If, in the days of a burgeoning population at Sparta, the *enomotia* was a larger unit of, perhaps, 45 men, then a smaller '30' might have proved useful on occasion; but by the time of the Peloponnesian War, when the *enomotia* was averaging 32 men, there would be no point in a separate unit of '30', and the *triekades* could be allowed to disappear.

Army organization: the army of the *morai*

It seems that the Spartan army underwent a change in organization at some point after the events of Thukydides' *History*, for we suddenly meet a unit called a *mora* in 403 BC (Xen., *Hell*. 2.4.31). In fact, Xenophon describes an army establishment of six *morai* ('divisions'): 'each of the hoplite *morai* has one *polemarchos*, four *lochagoi*, eight *pentekonteres*, and 16 *enomotarchoi*' (Xen., *Lak. pol.* 11.4), preserving the same chain of command, if not the same unit ratios, as in the previous 'obal' army.

The number of *morai* is certain, for Aristotle provides confirmation in another fragment of his lost *Spartan Constitution* (Frg. 540), preserved in the *Suda*: 'Aristotle says that there are six named *morai* and all Lakedaimonians are divided amongst the *morai*' (*Suda*, 1259). But some scholars have suggested that the text of Xenophon's *Spartan Constitution* should be altered to give two *lochoi* per *mora*, rather than four, based on later events. When the Thebans invaded Sparta in 362 BC, for example, Agesilaos was short-handed because 'three of the 12 *lochoi* were absent in Arkadia' (Xen., *Hell.* 7.5.10). On Xenophon's own reckoning, there ought to have been, not 12, but 24 *lochoi* in total, but there had perhaps been further changes in the wake of the disaster at Leuktra.

The *mora* appears to have been roughly the size of the 'obal' army's *lochos*, and suffered the same decline in numbers: the *mora* defeated at Lechaion in 390 BC numbered 'around 600' (Xen., *Hell.* 4.5.12), for example, while Agesilaos' five *morai* which invaded Boiotia in 378 BC 'each contained 500 men' (Diod. 15.32.1). This diminution need not imply a similar shrinking of the *enomotia*, but it is possible that its manpower now approached the *Suda*'s estimate of 25 men, making Xenophon's *pentekostys* roughly 50 or 60 men, which is half the size of the *pentekostyes* at Mantineia.

What was the reason for this change in army establishment? It may be linked with the manpower shortage at Sparta, which had probably, by now, obliged the Spartiates to admit *perioikoi* into their ranks, whereas they had previously served in separate regiments. They probably already fought side-by-side at Leuktra, but clearer evidence comes a few years later in 365 BC, when the Spartan garrison of Kromnos was captured by the Arkadians; although some men managed to escape, 'the total number of captured Spartiates and *perioikoi* came to more than 100' (Xen., *Hell.* 7.4.27).

On campaign

According to Spartan tradition, 'when the army took the field, the Kings go out first and return last' (Hdt. 6.56), but, from an early date, only one king at

Detail of the north frieze from the Siphnian Treasury at Delphi depicting the so-called 'Gigantomachy', or battle between the gods (advancing from left) and the giants, depicted as hoplites. The figure of Ares, god of war (centre), sports the beard and long hair of the Spartans. (Now in Delphi Museum. Wikimedia Commons/ Fingalo)

a time. Before embarking, the king 'first made an offering to Zeus Agetor ('the leader') and to the associated gods (i.e. the heavenly twins, Kastor and Polydeukes)' (Xen., *Lak. pol.* 13.2). If the omens were good, an official known as the *pyrphoros* ('fire-bearer') carried a lit torch to the Lakedaimonian border, where the king sacrificed once more. This was the so-called *diabateria*, or 'sacrifice at the frontier'. Only if the omens were favourable could the army leave the 'hollow land' on campaign; if they were bad, there was no option but to return home.

When the army finally set off, it was invariably accompanied by sheep and goats 'to serve as sacrifices to the gods and to give good omens before battle' (Paus. 9.13.4). Before the battle of Nemea in 394 BC, for example, 'when the armies were no more than a stade (around 200m) apart, the Lakedaimonians sacrificed a she-goat to Artemis Agrotera ('the huntress'), according to their laws, and led the charge against their adversaries' (Xen., *Hell.* 4.2.20). On this occasion, Artemis smiled upon the Spartans, who lost only eight men in the battle.

On campaign, each Spartan warrior was probably accompanied by one helot servant as a baggage carrier. Herodotos records that Eurytos, one of the two Spartiates whom Leonidas had excused from the battle line at Thermopylai on account of an eye complaint, was accompanied by a helot; likewise, Kleomenes' men at the battle of Sepeia in 494 BC, and the men on Sphakteria in 425 BC. Oddly, at Plataia, each Spartiate seems to have had seven helots, but even the former admiral Anaxibios was accompanied on campaign by a single helot (Xen., *Hell.* 4.8.39, referring to him as a *hypaspist*,

Greek red-figure *kylix*, *c.*500 BC, depicting the sacrifice of a young boar at an altar. (Now in the Louvre, Paris. Wikimedia Commons/Marie-Lan Nguyen)

or 'shield-bearer'). It may be no coincidence that, in 362 BC, King Agesilaos went to parley with the invading Thebans 'wearing his *himation* and accompanied by a single servant' (Plut., *Ages.* 32.4).

In battle, the *enomotiai* could be drawn up with various frontages, so that each must have had several men willing and able to serve as file-leaders. In fact, we get a flavour of Thukydides' 'officers commanding other officers' in the Sphakteria episode, where a certain Stryphon had been obliged to take command 'since, of the initial commanders, Epitadas, who was the first, had been killed, and Hippagretas, who had been chosen to succeed him, lay amongst the dead, although he was still alive' (Thuk. 4.38.1).

As Xenophon explains in his *Spartan Constitution*, 'in the Spartan battle-array, those standing in the front are officers, and every file has everything required to operate independently' (Xen., *Lak. pol.* 11.5). He denied that Spartan manoeuvres were complex, pointing out that, since every man ought to know his place, the moves were quite straightforward. 'However', he continues, 'the arrangement whereby, even if they are in disorder, they fight equally well with whomever happens to be next to them, is no longer easy to learn, except for those trained under the laws of Lykourgos' (11.7). This is surely a damning indictment of the 'army of the *morai*', where a Spartiate (being one of 'those trained under the laws of Lykourgos') could no longer guarantee that his neighbours in the battle-line were also staunch Spartiates.

BELIEF AND BELONGING

Spartan law

The exiled King Demaratos summarized the Spartan ethos for the benefit of the Persian King Xerxes: 'fighting singly, Spartans are no worse than other men, but together they are the most excellent of all warriors; for they are free, but not entirely free, because the Law is their master, whom they fear much more than your men fear you' (Hdt. 7.104.4). The Spartan warrior

THE BATTLEFIELD SACRIFICE AT PLATAIA, 479 BC

The critical battle of the Persian Wars was fought some way to the north-east of the town of Plataia. In the manoeuvring before the day of the battle, the Spartan Army led by the regent Pausanias (standing in for Leonidas' under-age son Pleistarchos) became separated from the other Greek contingents. The Persians then focused their attack on the Spartans, and subjected them to an archery barrage from behind a protective wall of wicker shields.

Having drawn up in line of battle, the Spartans could not engage until they had received a favourable omen from the *sphagia*. This was a special, pre-battle sacrifice that did not involve altars or fires, but seems simply to have relied upon the priests observing the flow of blood from the animal's throat (*sphage*). Herodotos records that 'the *sphagia* was producing no favourable result, and all the time many of the Spartans were dying and far more were being wounded, for the Persians were freely shooting showers of arrows from behind their wicker shields' (Hdt. 9.61.3).

It was customary for the rites to be performed by seers called *manteis* (sing. *mantis*), whose speciality was interpreting signs. However, at such a critical moment, their divination was surely a mere formality, and it has been suggested that Pausanias (shown standing with helmet pushed back to observe the proceedings) deliberately prolonged the *sphagia*, either to build false confidence in the Persians or to await the arrival of his Athenian allies. In his *Life of Aristeides* (the commander of the Athenian forces in the battle), Plutarch describes the Spartan priests' staves and scourges, imagining that they were used to beat back the enemy, but there is no mention of this in Herodotos' account.

Ivory plaques from Sparta. At bottom left, the goddess Artemis appears as Agrotera, 'the huntress'; at bottom right, she appears as the winged Orthia, 'the healer'. (Now in the National Archaeological Museum, Athens. Photo © Stefanos Skarmintzos)

was governed by one overriding principle: 'The Spartans do whatever the Law commands, and it always commands the same thing: not to flee from battle, even against overwhelming numbers, but to remain in the ranks and either prevail or perish.' (Hdt. 7.104.5)

Anyone who did not abide by this principle brought disgrace upon himself and suffered the dishonour of being labelled a *tresas* ('runaway'). This was a serious offence at Sparta; such a coward was no longer welcome in the communal *syssition*; he was doomed to wear a shabby *tribon* and shave half of his *hypene*. Worse still, he lost his citizen status as a Spartiate and was obliged to defer to his juniors in all matters. 'I am not surprised', writes Xenophon, 'that they prefer death to a life so filled with dishonour and disgrace' (Xen., *Lak. pol.* 9.6).

Although a man who fled the field of battle might be accused of *atimia* (literally, 'lack of honour'), his offence was compounded if he had failed to protect the king. A king had fallen at Thermopylai in 480 BC, another at Leuktra in 371 BC, and another at Megalopolis in 331 BC. There, the dying King Agis instructed his men 'to withdraw as quickly as possible and save themselves for the needs of the fatherland' (Diod. 17.63.4). Equally, after Leuktra, Agesilaos famously waived the penalty for the 300 or so Spartiates who had survived the battle, 'declaring that the laws must be allowed to sleep for the day' (Plut., *Ages.* 30.2–4; also *Ap. Bas.*, *Ages.* 10 = *Mor.* 191C). But his decision, like Agis', had been forced on him by the needs of Sparta and her desperate decline in population.

The disgrace of the Spartans who surrendered on Sphakteria in 425 BC was not as great, no king having been lost. Yet, on their return to Sparta in 421 BC, they suffered *atimia*, 'such that they should neither hold a command nor have the authority to buy or sell' (Thuk. 5.34.2). However, their punishment was soon lifted.

Aristodemos 'the runaway' was not so fortunate; when he missed the battle of Thermopylai owing to an eye disease, and returned home as the sole survivor, 'he was deprived of honour in this way: none of the Spartiates would give him fire or speak to him' (Hdt. 7.231). Nevertheless, his punishment must also have been lifted, for he fought at Plataia in the following year, where he demonstrated in no uncertain terms that his condemnation as a *tresas* had been unjust; he was killed, 'raging and running out from the battle-line to achieve great deeds' (Hdt. 9.71). By contrast, the two *polemarchoi*, Aristokles and Hipponoidas, who failed to manoeuvre their troops as they had been ordered at Mantineia, 'on account of this offence were banished from Sparta because they were held guilty of cowardice' (Thuk. 5.72.1).

Spartan loyalty

The Spartan warrior's first loyalty was to Sparta. When the army was on campaign, the womenfolk invariably asked for news, not of their husbands or sons, but of how the country was faring (e.g. Plut., *Lak. Ap.*, *Anon. 5, 7 = Mor.* 241B, C). It was a well-known Spartan maxim that men were born to die for Sparta. The epitaph to the fallen at Thermopylai makes this clear: 'Tell the Lakedaimonians, stranger, that here we lie, obeying their customs' (Hdt. 7.228.2).

We have seen that fighting to the death was part of the Spartan ethos. The surviving fragments of Tyrtaios' poetry glorify battle: 'to fall and die amongst those fighting in the front is a beautiful thing for a brave man who is doing battle on behalf of his country' (Tyrt. Frg. 10). A later fragment sums up the Spartans' martial fraternity: 'Those who dare to remain in their place at one another's side and advance together towards hand-to-hand combat and those fighting in the front, they die in lesser numbers, and they save the army behind them; but when men flee in terror, all soldierly excellence is lost.' (Tyrt. Frg. 11, lines 11–14)

Xenophon believed that this attitude – 'that an honourable death was preferable to a life of disgrace' (Xen., *Lak. pol.* 9.1) – was inculcated in the Spartiates. Furthermore, their obedience to authority was generally second nature. 'We all know', writes Xenophon, 'that, most of all in Sparta, they obey their magistrates and the laws' (Xen., *Lak. pol.* 8.1). Of course, their laws were considered sacrosanct because they had come from the divine oracle of Apollo at Delphi; disobedience was doubly damning, as it incurred impiety and dishonour.

Spartan religion

The Spartans were deeply religious, as we have seen from the various rituals of the army on campaign. Herodotos, for one, believed that 'the things of the god they deem more important than the things of man' (Hdt. 5.63.2). It seems that their Argive neighbours were wise to all of the Spartans' religious foibles. In 419 BC, when an Argive quarrel with pro-Spartan Epidauros was brewing, King Agis marched out on the eve of the Karneia festival, but received bad omens and had to stand down. The Argives knew that, once the religious

Ivory votive plaques of the goddess Artemis from the Sanctuary of Artemis Orthia at Sparta. In her guise as the huntress, she was worshipped as a warlike deity. (Now in the National Archaeological Museum, Athens. Wikimedia Commons/Marsyas)

festival had begun, the Spartans could not stir forth, so they promptly invaded and plundered Epidauros with impunity.

The Argives were particularly skilful at manipulating Spartan religious scruple. In 417 BC, for example, they waited until the Spartans were celebrating the religious festival of Gymnopaidiai before ousting the pro-Spartan party at Argos. However, the Argives' strategy did not always succeed. In 388 BC, they attempted to forestall a Spartan invasion by bringing forward their sacred month, hoping that King Agesipolis would hesitate to break a sacred truce. However, Agesipolis sought and received permission from the oracles at Olympia and Delphi, and freely proceeded to ravage Argolis, until subsequent omens taken after a thunderstorm reversed his decision.

Burial of the dead

The influence of religion continued after the battle. Some city-states scrupulously repatriated their war-dead, but the Spartan oath called for Spartiates to be buried where they had fallen. Or, in practice, in the nearest allied territory to the battlefield. For example, after the battle of Mantineia in 418 BC, the Spartans 'took up their dead and carried them off to Tegea where they buried them' (Thuk. 5.74.2). Similarly, after Lysander and his men fell at the battle of Haliartos in 395 BC, the regent Pausanias, arriving too late for the battle, concluded a truce so that the bodies could be gathered up; then, 'as soon as they were beyond the boundary of Boiotia carrying Lysander's body, they buried him in the country of the Panopeans, their friends and allies' (Plut., *Lys.* 29.3).

Greek black-figure *kylix* by the so-called 'Hunt Painter' (*c.*550–530 BC), depicting Spartan warriors carrying their dead comrades from the battlefield. Now in the Altes Museum, Berlin. (© Karwansaray Publishers, courtesy of Jasper Oorthuys)

In fact, Spartan war graves became permanent markers of Spartan involvement on foreign soil; they had contrived to leave a little piece of Sparta in the territories of their allies, as a reminder of their good faith. In 427 BC, when the long-besieged Plataians finally surrendered their town to the Spartans, they begged for clemency on the grounds that they had tended the

The Tomb of the Lakedaimonians in the Kerameikos cemetery at Athens, viewed from the north-west, looking in the direction of the Akropolis. (Author's collection)

Spartan war grave from the battle of 479 BC 'with garments and other customary offerings, and as much of the harvest as our land produced' (Thuk. 3.58.4).

Most intriguing of all is the 'Tomb of the Lakedaimonians' at Athens, which contains the casualties from the Spartan army sent to support the Athenian oligarchy during the civil strife which followed Athens' defeat in the Peloponnesian War. Excavation of the mass grave by the Deutsches Archäologisches Institut in the 1930s revealed 23 battle-scarred skeletons interred in separate compartments, some in groups and some individually; the latter presumably included the two *polemarchoi* and other high status individuals whom Xenophon names (Xen., *Hell.* 2.4.33). The skeletons were found to have been wrapped, probably in their red cloaks as prescribed by Lykourgos (Plut., *Lyk.* 27.1–2; *Inst. Lac.* 18 = *Mor.* 238D), and laid out with each man's head resting on a stone.

Lykourgos was believed to have 'abolished the inscriptions on memorials, except for those who had fallen in war' (Plut., *Inst. Lac.* 18 = *Mor.* 238D). In fact, some two dozen of these *mnemeia* ('memorials') are known from the vicinity of Sparta, commemorating men who died 'in war'. Given the Spartan tradition of burial near the battlefield, they surely do not mark the men's graves. On the contrary, the stele of a certain Eualkes discovered at Geraki, to the south-east of Sparta, unusually carries the extra information 'at Mantineia' after the standard formula 'in war'. If Eualkes fell in the battle of 418 BC, his body will have been buried with his comrades at Tegea.

Grave stele from Pellana, on the road from Sparta to Arkadia, with typically laconic inscription. It reads simply *Olbiadas en polemoi*, meaning 'Olbiadas, (who died) in war'. (Now in Sparta Museum. Photo © Stefanos Skarmintzos)

THE BATTLE OF KORONEIA, 394 BC

A Theban-led coalition of troops, including Athenians, Argives and Corinthians, met Agesilaos' Spartans and their Phokian allies (reinforced by a body of *neodamodeis* and the remnants of Xenophon's 'Ten Thousand' mercenaries) at Koroneia in Boiotia. In the ensuing clash, the Argives, who were positioned opposite the Spartans, turned and fled, but the Thebans, who were positioned on the other flank, broke through the Phokians and began plundering Agesilaos' baggage park.

At this, Agesilaos, 'immediately countermarching his phalanx, led it against them' (Xen., *Hell.* 4.3.18). Xenophon's brief statement conceals the fact that the Spartans had executed the complicated manoeuvre known as *anastrophe*, or 'turning backwards', in which each file of men snaked back through the phalanx to create its mirror image facing in the opposite direction. Crucially, the original file-leaders remained in the front rank, and the original file-closers remained at the rear.

Xenophon comments that the Spartans could easily have allowed the Thebans to pass by, which would have left them vulnerable to a flank or rear attack, but a head-on meeting of phalanxes was more honourable. 'Crashing their shields together', writes Xenophon, who was probably present at the battle, 'they shoved, they struggled, they slew, and they died' (Xen., *Hell.* 4.3.19).

The Spartans are shown in the act of countermarching, with each *enomotia* at a different stage of the manoeuvre, to illustrate the process. The Thebans are shown heading for the Spartan baggage park. They are depicted with the 'club of Herakles' motif on their shields; the same symbol appears on vase paintings and on Boiotian coins, and Xenophon implies that it was their state symbol (Xen., *Hell.* 7.5.20). By contrast, the evidence for a Spartan state symbol is problematic, and it seems likely that their shields were left plain.

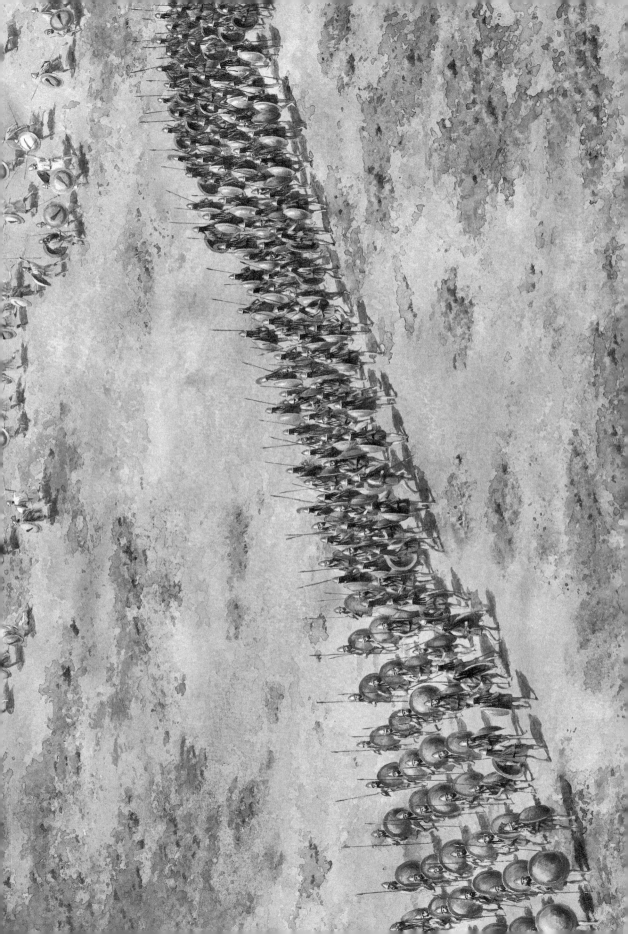

THE WARRIOR IN BATTLE

The Spartan warriors were famously disciplined on the battlefield. They regularly marched into battle slowly, to the sound of many pipes, 'so that, walking evenly and regularly, their ranks would not become disjointed' (Thuk. 5.70); the overall effect was to broadcast an eerie calm. Agesilaos had even managed to withdraw his phalanx from battle in good order, utilizing the manoeuvre known as *anastrophe*, or 'turning backwards' (Xen., *Hell.* 6.5.18–19), whereby the men faced about where they stood and marched through the ranks to the rear, so that the same file leaders were still at the front.

However, the declining numbers of Spartiates led to the gradual adulteration of the ranks, with hoplites drawn from the *perioikoi* and *neodamodeis*; the army became truly Lakedaimonian, rather than purely Spartan. These men did not share the total immersion in military training experienced by the Spartan warrior, and it is telling that Xenophon wrote about how the unflinching obedience of the Spartiates should prevail even when the army is in disorder.

Of course, battles are won by good generalship, but morale plays a considerable part. The events of the battle of Tegyra in 375 BC illustrate how much the Spartan army had changed, no doubt owing to the decline of the purely Spartiate, oath-bound *enomotiai*: when two 500-strong Lakedaimonian *morai* stumbled upon 300 Theban hoplites under the command of Pelopidas, we might imagine that the roles had been reversed, for it was the Thebans who acted like the Spartans of old, and the Lakedaimonians who broke and fled as soon as their *polemarchoi* were killed (Plut., *Pel.* 17.1–4).

It is ironic that, as the ranks of the pure-bred Spartan warriors thinned and their influence on the Spartan army was diluted, their proverbial excellence was finally eclipsed by an enemy (the Thebans at Leuktra) who adopted the key principles of obedience and orderliness in battle. The days had passed, when 'if you watch carefully, you might consider all others improvisers in soldiering, and only the Spartans craftsmen in warfare' (Xen., *Lak. pol.* 13.5).

Modern statue of King Leonidas, erected in 1968 at Sparta. According to Plutarch, at Thermopylai in 480 BC, when the Persian King Xerxes demanded that the Spartans surrender their weapons, Leonidas replied: *molon labe* – 'Come and get them'. (Wikimedia Commons/Gonzalo Serrano Espada)

G **AFTER THE BATTLE OF MANTINEIA, 418 BC**

After a battle, it was customary to collect the dead for burial. However, the victor had the right to strip the vanquished corpses and erect a victory trophy symbolizing possession of the battlefield. The defeated side acknowledged their defeat by formally requesting permission to retrieve their fallen for decent burial.

At Mantineia, Thukydides records that the Spartans 'grounded their arms' in front of the enemy dead, thus compelling the Argives and their allies to seek formal permission for their repatriation. 'The Lakedaimonians immediately set up a trophy and stripped the dead' (Thuk. 5.74.2). The trophy was intended as an offering of thanks to the gods. It consisted of captured arms and armour draped on a pole or a convenient tree trunk as a makeshift mannequin, 'so that the memorials of hostility would last only for a brief time and quickly disappear' (Diod. 13.24.6).

Shortly afterwards, the Spartans took up their own dead and, as was their custom, buried them close to the battlefield in the nearest allied territory; on this occasion, burial took place some way to the south, in the land of their Tegean allies. The Spartans took a very businesslike attitude to battle, so there were no elaborate victory celebrations. Indeed, Plutarch records that the man who brought news of the victory at Mantineia to Sparta received nothing for his trouble, except 'a piece of meat sent by the ephors from their *syssition*' (Plut., *Ages.* 33.4).

FURTHER READING

Original source material is available in translation in the Loeb, Penguin Classics and Oxford World Classics series. In addition, Herodotos, Thukydides and Xenophon's *Hellenika* are all available in Robert Strassler's highly recommended 'Landmark' series.

J. F. Lazenby's *The Spartan Army* is fundamental, and should be read alongside the reviews of Manfred Clauss (*Gnomon*, Vol. 58.4, 1986, pp. 309–13), Thomas J. Figueira (*Classical World*, Vol. 80.3, 1987, pp. 214–15), W. G. Forrest (*Journal of Hellenic Studies*, Vol. 107, 1987, p. 231), and Stephen Hodkinson (*Classical Review*, Vol. 36.2, 1986, pp. 327–28).

Readers may also find much of interest in the occasional proceedings of the International Sparta Seminar, most of which have been edited by Stephen Hodkinson and Anton Powell and published by the Classical Press of Wales. The *Sparta & War* volume (see Hodkinson & Powell 2006 below) is particularly relevant.

The world of the Spartan warrior

Billheimer, A., 'Ta deka aph'hebes', *Transactions and Proceedings of the American Philological Association*, Vol. 77 (Baltimore, 1946), pp. 214–20

——, 'Age-classes in Spartan education', *Transactions and Proceedings of the American Philological Association*, Vol. 78 (Baltimore, 1947), pp. 99–104

David, E., 'Sparta's social hair', *Eranos*, Vol. 90 (Uppsala, 1992), pp. 11–21

——, 'Sparta and the politics of nudity', in Powell & Hodkinson (2010), pp. 137–63

Ducat, J., 'The Spartan "tremblers"', in Hodkinson & Powell (2006), pp. 1–55

——, *Spartan education: youth and society in the classical period* (Swansea, 2006)

Figueira, T. J., 'Mess contributions and subsistence at Sparta', *Transactions of the American Philological Association*, Vol. 114 (Baltimore, 1984), pp. 87–109

——, 'Population patterns in Late Archaic and Classical Sparta', *Transactions of the American Philological Association*, Vol. 116 (Baltimore, 1986), pp. 165–213

——, (ed.), *Spartan Society* (Swansea, 2004)

——, 'The nature of the Spartan *kleros*', in Figueira (2004), pp. 47–76

——, 'The Spartan *hippeis*', in Hodkinson & Powell (2006), pp. 57–84

Flower, M. A., 'Spartan "religion" and Greek "religion"', in Hodkinson (2009), pp. 193–229

Grundy, G. B., 'The population and policy of Sparta in the fifth century', *Journal of Hellenic Studies*, Vol. 28 (London, 1908), pp. 77–96

Hammond, M., 'A famous *exemplum* of Spartan toughness', *Classical Journal*, Vol. 75.2 (Minneapolis, 1980), pp. 97–109

Hodkinson, S., 'Land tenure and inheritance in Classical Sparta', *Classical Quarterly*, Vol. 36.2 (Cambridge, 1986), pp. 378–406

——, 'Social order and the conflict of values in Classical Sparta', *Chiron*, Vol. 13 (Munich, 1983), pp. 241–65

——, (ed.), *Sparta: Comparative Approaches* (Swansea, 2009)

——, & Powell A., (eds.), *Sparta: New Perspectives* (London, 1999)

——, & Powell A., (eds.), *Sparta and War* (Swansea, 2006)

Hornblower, S., 'Sticks, stones, and Spartans: the sociology of Spartan violence', in H. van Wees (ed.), *War and Violence in Ancient Greece* (London, 2000), pp. 57–82

Link, S., 'Education and pederasty in Spartan and Cretan society', in Hodkinson (2009), pp. 89–111

Low, P., 'Commemorating the Spartan war-dead', in Hodkinson & Powell (2006), pp. 85–109

Luraghi, N., 'Helotic slavery reconsidered', in Powell & Hodkinson (2002), pp. 227-266

Millender, E., 'The Spartan dyarchy: a comparative perspective', in Hodkinson (2009), pp. 1–67

Powell, A. & Hodkinson S. (eds.), *Sparta: Beyond the Mirage* (London, 2002)

——, (eds.), *Sparta: The Body Politic* (Swansea, 2010)

Singor, H. W., 'Admission to the *syssitia* in fifth-century Sparta', in Hodkinson & Powell (1999), pp. 67–89

Tazelaar, C. M., '*Paides kai epheboi*: Some notes on the Spartan stages of youth', *Mnemosyne*, Vol. 20.2 (Leiden, 1967), pp. 127–53

Thomas, C. G., 'On the role of the Spartan kings', *Historia*, Vol. 23.3 (Stuttgart, 1974), pp. 257–70

Toynbee, A. J., 'The Growth of Sparta', *Journal of Hellenic Studies*, Vol. 33 (London, 1913), pp. 246–75

Wade-Gery, H. T., 'The Spartan Rhetra in Plutarch, *Lycurgus VI*: C. What is the Rhetra?', *Classical Quarterly*, Vol. 38.3/4 (Cambridge, 1944), pp. 115–26

Willetts, R. F., 'The Neodamodeis', *Classical Philology*, Vol. 49 (Chicago, 1954), pp. 27–32

Hoplite equipment and Spartan warfare

Anderson, J. K., *Military Theory and Practice in the Age of Xenophon* (Berkeley, 1970)

——, 'Sickle and *Xyele*', *Journal of Hellenic Studies*, Vol. 94 (London, 1974), p. 166

Blyth, P. H., 'The structure of a hoplite shield in the Museo Gregoriano Etrusco', *Bollettino Monumenti, Musei e Gallerie Pontificie*, Vol. 3 (Vatican City, 1982), pp. 5–21

Cartledge, P., 'Hoplites and heroes: Sparta's contribution to the technique of ancient warfare', *Journal of Hellenic Studies*, Vol. 97 (London, 1977), pp. 11–27

Humble, N., 'Why the Spartans fight so well, even if they are in disorder – Xenophon's view', in Hodkinson & Powell (2006), pp. 219–33

Kelly, D. H., 'Thucydides and Herodotus on the Pitanate *Lochos*', *Greek, Roman and Byzantine Studies*, Vol. 22.1 (Durham, 1981), pp. 31–38

Lazenby, J. F., *The Spartan Army* (Warminster, 1985)

——, & D. Whitehead, 'The myth of the hoplite's *hoplon*', *Classical Quarterly*, Vol. 46.1 (Cambridge, 1996), pp. 27–33

Lorimer, T. J., 'The hoplite phalanx with special reference to the poems of Archilochus and Tyrtaeus', *Annual of the British School at Athens*, Vol. 42 (London, 1947), pp. 76–138

Lupi, M., 'Amomphoretos, the *lochos* of Pitane and the Spartan system of villages', in Hodkinson & Powell (2006), pp. 185–218

Schwartz, A., *Reinstating the Hoplite: Arms, armour and phalanx fighting in Archaic and Classical Greece* (Stuttgart, 2009)

Singor, H. W., 'The Spartan army at Mantinea and its organisation in the fifth century BC', in W. Jongman & M. Kleijwegt (eds.), *After the Past. Essays in ancient history in honour of H.W. Pleket* (Leiden, 2002), pp. 235–84

Van Wees, H., '"The Oath of the Sworn Bands": The Acharnae stela, the Oath of Plataea and archaic Spartan warfare', in A. Luther & M. Meer (eds.), *Das Frühe Sparta* (Stuttgart, 2006), pp. 125–64

GLOSSARY

agele	(**pl.** *agelai)* band (literally 'herd') of Spartan boys during their training period, similar to the *ile* (q.v.); the members of each *agele* are thought to have been drawn from the same age group
agoge	training regime (literally 'guidance') followed by all male Spartans between the ages of seven and 30, sometimes translated as 'the upbringing'
choinix	(**pl.** *choinikes)* unit of dry measure, equating to one man's daily allowance of barley meal; ¼₈ of a *medimnos* (q.v.)
chous	(**pl.** *choes)* unit of liquid measure, sometimes translated as 'pitcher'; at Sparta, on analogy with the *medimnos* (q.v.), it probably equated to roughly one-and-a-half times the 3-litre Attic *chous*
diabateria	the official sacrifice at the Lakedaimonian frontier (literally 'crossing the border'), made before every campaign
eiren	(**pl.** *eirenes)* young Spartan aged 20, in his first year as a *hebon* (q.v.)
ekklesia	the assembly of all Spartiates (q.v.), which met monthly on the feast day of Apollo
enomotia	(**pl.** *enomotiai)* military unit commanded by an *enomotarches* (q.v.); smallest subdivision of the Spartan army, derived from the adjective *enomotos*, 'bound by oath'
enomotarches	(**pl.** *enomotarchai)* commander of an *enomotia* (q.v.)
ephor	one of five annually-appointed magistrates; the Greek word *ephoros* (pl. *ephoroi*) means 'supervisor'
erastes	(**pl.** *erastai)* the Spartan boy's 'admirer', perhaps roughly ten years older than him
Gerousia	council of 28 elders, elected for life
geron	(**pl.** *gerontes)* elder Spartan, aged 60 or over, eligible for election to the *Gerousia* (q.v.)
hebon	(**pl.** *hebontes)* Spartan youth, aged between 20 and 29
helot	Spartan serf; the Greek word *heilotes* (pl. *heilotai*) perhaps derives from the verb *heilon*, 'to capture'
hippagretas	(**pl.** *hippagretai)* one of three Spartiates selected each year as (literally) 'choosers of the *hippeis*', each responsible for picking 100 *hippeis* (q.v.)

hippeis	(**sing.** *hippeus*) royal bodyguard of 300 Spartans, annually selected from the *hebontes* (q.v.)
homoios	(**pl.** *homoioi*) full Spartan citizen (literally 'equal'), synonymous with Spartiate (q.v.)
hypomeion	(**pl.** *hypomeiones*) Spartan citizens of inferior status, mentioned only by Xenophon
ile	(**pl.** *ilai*) band (literally 'crowd') of Spartan boys, similar to the *agele* (q.v.)
kleros	(**pl.** *kleroi*) allotment of land owned by a Spartan citizen
kotyle	(**pl.** *kotylai*) liquid measure, sometimes translated as 'cupful'; $\frac{1}{12}$ of a *chous* (q.v.)
lochagos	(**pl.** *lochagoi*) commander (literally 'company leader') of a *lochos* (q.v.)
lochos	(**pl.** *lochoi*) regiment of the Spartan army, commanded by a *lochagos* (q.v.)
medimnos	(**pl.** *medimnoi*) unit of dry measure, sometimes translated as 'bushel'; at Sparta, it seems to have equated to roughly one-and-a-half times the standard 52-litre Attic *medimnos*
melleiren	(**pl.** *melleirenes*) Spartan *paidiskos* (q.v.), aged 18 or 19 (literally 'nearly an *eiren*'); the equivalent of the *ephebos* ('ephebe') of other Greek city-states
mina	(**pl.** *minai*) unit of weight, sometimes translated as 'pound'; roughly equivalent to 0.44kg
mora	(**pl.** *morai*) division of the Spartan army commanded by a *polemarchos* (q.v.)
neodamodes	(**pl.** *neodamodeis*) enfranchised helot, able to serve as a hoplite (literally 'new man of the people')
oba	(**pl.** *obai*) one of the five villages of Sparta
paidiskos	(**pl.** *paidiskoi*) Spartan boy, aged between (probably) 12 and 19 (see also *melleiren*)
paidonomos	(**pl.** *paidonomoi*) warden (literally 'herder of boys') in charge of Spartans during their training period, i.e. between the ages of seven and 30
pais	(**pl.** *paides)* Spartan boy, aged between seven and (probably) 12
pentekonter	(**pl.** *pentekonteres*) commander of a *pentekostys* (q.v.); the name seems to imply command over 50 men

pentekostys	(**pl.** *pentekostyes*) military unit commanded by a *pentekonter* (q.v.) and comprising four (later, two) *enomotiai* (q.v.)
perioikoi (**pl.**)	non-Spartan inhabitants of Lakedaimon (literally 'those who live round about')
polemarchos	(**pl.** *polemarchoi*) senior officer (literally 'war leader'); later, commander of a *mora* (q.v.)
Spartiate	Spartan citizen; the Greek word *Spartiates* (pl. *Spartiatai*) properly refers to the pure-bred Spartan who has completed the *agoge* (q.v.) and has achieved election to a *syssition* (q.v.); see also *homoios*
syssition	(**pl.** *syssitia*) 'mess-group', to which every Spartiate had to be elected and to which his household had to contribute
taxiarchos	(**pl.** *taxiarchoi*) Spartan officer (literally 'unit leader'), mentioned only by Herodotos
tresas	(**pl.** *tresantes*) Spartan disgraced for cowardice (literally 'runaway'), sometimes translated as 'trembler'
triekas	(**pl.** *triekades*) unit of Spartan army (literally '30'), mentioned only by Herodotos

ABBREVIATIONS

Ar., *Acharn.*	Aristophanes, *Acharneis* (*Acharnians*)
Ar., *Hipp.*	Aristophanes, *Hippeis* (*Knights*)
Arist., *Hist. An.*	Aristotle, *Peri ta Zoia Historion* (commonly rendered *Historia Animalium*, or *History of Animals*)
Arist., *Pol.*	Aristotle, *Politika* (*The Politics*)
Arist., *Rhet.*	Aristotle, *Techne Rhetorike* (*The Art of Rhetoric*)
Athen., *Deipn.*	Athenaeus, *Deipnosophistai* (*The Learned Banqueters*)
Cic., *Flacc.*	Cicero, *Pro Flacco* (*In Defence of Lucius Flaccus*)
Diod.	Diodorus Siculus (*The Library of History*)
Hdt.	Herodotos (*The Histories*)
Paus.	Pausanias (*Description of Greece*)
Pl., *Leg.*	Plato, *Nomoi* (commonly rendered as *Leges*, or *The Laws*)
Plut., *Ages.*	Plutarch, *Agesilaos* (*Life of Agesilaus*)

Plut., *Alk.*	Plutarch, *Alkibiades* (*Life of Alcibiades*)
Plut., *Ap. Bas.*	Plutarch, *Apophthegmata Basileon kai Strategon* (*Sayings of Kings and Commanders*), catalogued chronologically, kings first, then commanders (*Epam.* = *Epameinondas*)
Plut., *Ap. Lak.*	Plutarch, *Apophthegmata Lakonika* (*Sayings of Spartans*), catalogued by their supposed source (*Ages.* = *Agesilaos*, *Agis* = *Agis the Younger*, *Ant.* = *Antalkidas*, *Bras.* = *Brasidas*, *Dem.* = *Demaratos*, *Lyk.* = *Lykourgos*, *Khar.* = *Kharillos*, *Anon.* = unknown)
Plut., *De san.*	Plutarch, *Hygieina Parangelmata* (*Advice About Keeping Well*, sometimes rendered as *De tuenda sanitate praecepta*)
Plut., *Inst. Lac.*	Plutarch, *Palaia Epitedeumata ton Lakedaimonion* (*Ancient Customs of the Spartans*, sometimes rendered as *Instituta Laconica*)
Plut., *Kim.*	Plutarch, *Kimon* (*Life of Cimon*)
Plut., *Kleom.*	Plutarch, *Kleomenes* (*Life of Cleomenes*)
Plut., *Lak. Ap.*	Plutarch, *Lakainon Apophthegmata* (*Sayings of Spartan Women*), catalogued by their supposed source (*Anon.* = unknown)
Plut., *Lyk.*	Plutarch, *Lykourgos* (*Life of Lycurgus*)
Plut., *Lys.*	Plutarch, *Lysandros* (*Life of Lysander*)
Plut., *Mor.*	Plutarch, *Moralia* (a selection of short philosophical works)
Plut., *Pel.*	Plutarch, *Pelopidas* (*Life of Pelopidas*)
Poll.	Pollux (*Onomasticon*)
Thuk.	Thukydides (*A History of the Peloponnesian War*)
Tyrt.	Tyrtaios
Val. Max.	Valerius Maximus (*Memorable Deeds and Sayings*)
Xen., *Ages.*	Xenophon, *Agesilaos* (*Life of Agesilaus*)
Xen., *Hell.*	Xenophon, *Hellenika* (*History of Greek Affairs*, sometimes translated as *A History of my Times*)
Xen., *Lak. pol.*	Xenophon, *Lakedaimonion politeia* (*Spartan Constitution*; the authorship is sometimes disputed, though not the general date)
Xen., *Mem.*	Xenophon, *Apomnemoneumata* (commonly rendered as *Memorabilia*, or more rarely as *Conversations with Socrates*)

INDEX

References to illustrations are shown in **bold**